HABITUDES™

IMAGES
THAT FORM
LEADERSHIP
HABITS &
ATTITUDES

BY

DR TIM
ELMORE

My special thanks to Keith Drury, who inspired

many of the images you'll find in this series of

books. Keith was the first person who taught me

leadership principles through the power of pictures.

Thanks, Keith, for being such a good mentor.

I want to dedicate this book to my mother—

who modeled great relationships and leadership

all her life. She set the standard for me.

PUBLISHED IN ATLANTA, GEORGIA BY GROWING LEADERS, INC.
(WWW.GROWINGLEADERS.COM)

ISBN: 0-9792940-1-0
PRINTED IN THE UNITED STATES OF AMERICA
LIBRARY OF CONGRESS CATALOGUING-IN-PUBLICATION DATA

TABLE OF CONTENTS

A WORD ABOUT IMAGES

We live in a culture rich with images. We grew up with photographs, TV, movies, video, MTV, and DVDs. We can't escape the power of the visual image—and most of us don't want to.

I've learned over my career that most of us are visual learners. We like to see a picture, not just hear a word. Author Leonard Sweet says that images are the language of the 21st century, not words. Some of the best communicators in history taught using the power of the metaphor and image. One example is Martin Luther King, Jr. and his "I Have a Dream" speech, during the Civil Rights movement. Tom Peters once wrote, "The best leaders… almost without exception and at every level, are master users of stories and symbols."

Why? Because pictures stick. We remember pictures long after words have left us. When we hear a speech, we often remember the stories from that speech more than the phrases used by the speaker because they painted a picture inside of us. Pictures communicate far more than mere words. In fact, words are helpful only as they conjure up a picture in our minds. Most of us think in pictures. If I say the word "elephant" to you, you don't picture the letters e-l-e-p-h-a-n-t. You picture a big gray animal. Pictures are what we file away in our minds. They enable us to store huge volumes of information. There's an old phrase that has stood the test of time: A picture is worth a thousand words. I pursued a degree in both commercial art as well as theology in college. That's when I recognized the power of the image. Now I get to combine the power of teaching leadership principles with the power of pictures. I hope they linger in your mind and heart. I hope you discover layers of reality in them as you grow. I trust they'll impact you as profoundly as they have me.

This book is about personal power as opposed to positional power. You influence others best when you don't have to leverage your position to do so. Instead, you harness your personal power in the relationship. The book is designed to furnish pictures you can discuss with a community of people. I encourage you to go through the series in a group. Each picture contains layers of reality, and your discussion can go as deep as you allow it to go.

This series was created to guide you on your leadership journey. These books are based on the fact that leadership isn't merely one-dimensional—it runs 360 degrees. We influence others all around us. We must first lead ourselves. Then, we will also influence those above us. Next, we will influence those around us. Finally, we influence those for whom we are responsible. This book covers the art of connecting with others. Once I lead myself well, others should be magnetically attracted to follow. At this point, I must learn to connect with others through personal power. I become their friend and earn the right to be followed by assuming responsibility for the health of my relationships. Through the power of images, this book will enable you to discuss principles that will help you develop people through the power of good people skills.

Some sociologists describe this generation as EPIC: Experiential, Participatory, Image-driven, and Connected. If that's true, I believe we'll get the most out of resources that give us an image, an experience, and a way to connect with each other. Each of these books provides you not only with an image, but with a handful of discussion questions, a self-assessment, and an exercise in which you can participate. Dive in and experience each one of them. My hope is that they become signposts that guide you, warn you, and inform you on your leadership journey.

Dr. Tim Elmore

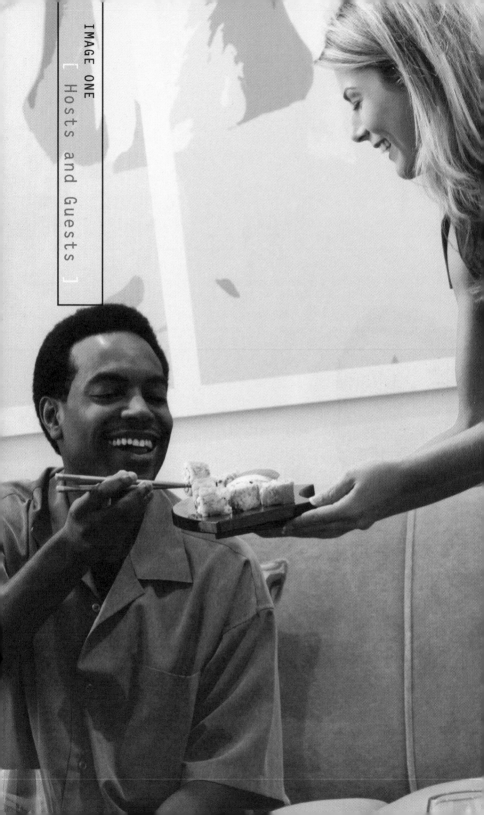

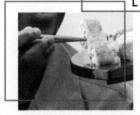

Hosts and Guests

LEADERS TAKE THE INITIATIVE IN RELATIONSHIPS. THEY ARE INTENTIONAL ABOUT THEM. THEY SEE THEMSELVES AS HOSTS, NOT GUESTS, AND GO OUT OF THEIR WAY TO CONNECT WITH PEOPLE AND PROVIDE FOR THEM.

While attending a university in London years ago, one young man accepted employment in East Africa. He began his venture there, curious to learn all he could about life, work and faith. For seven months he lived with a family where he hoped to be mentored in these areas.

Unfortunately, they were apathetic toward him. They never modeled the faith they claimed to have and never helped him get settled in Africa. He observed that the family was casual about their commitments in general. The student later claimed he learned what not to do from this family rather than what to do in life. Within a couple of months, he was disappointed in the whole experience. Eventually he moved back home to India, and ultimately, he led a revolution. This young man's name was Mahatma Gandhi.

That family in Africa had no idea who was in their midst. What an opportunity the family missed to influence Gandhi, one of the most influential men of the 20th century—because they were poor hosts. They never attempted to connect with him on any level.

You know what a good host looks like, don't you? If I was your friend and I came to visit you, I bet you'd know what to do to be a good host. After answering the door, I bet you'd invite me in, offer me a seat, take my coat, etc. A good host is someone who takes initiative, makes others feel comfortable, and connects. Most of us appreciate a good host, and we feel it when one is missing. Have you ever been in a room full of people and felt completely out of place? No one greeted you, showed you around, or even asked if you wanted something to drink. You probably thought about leaving, just like Gandhi. A good host would have made all the difference.

Parties aren't the only place you'll find hosts and guests. I've noticed nearly every relationship and every conversation has both a "host" and a "guest." People seem to find their place in discussions as either the proactive guide (the host), or the one responding (the guest). Now here's the catch. Most people view themselves as "guests" in life. They expect others to make the first move. Leaders know better. They take initiative and think like "hosts." Their focus isn't on themselves, but on others. In fact, when it comes to relationships, the first step a leader takes is to become a host, not a guest, wherever they are. This is rule number one. Good leaders don't depend on their position to get the job done. They leverage personal power, not positional power, with people.

It's been said that "some folks make you feel at home, while others make you wish you were." If you want to be a great "host" in relationships, you'll need to do the following things:

1. INITIATE (others become responsive)

2. CONNECT (others become comfortable)

3. PROVIDE (others become satisfied)

4. DIRECT (others receive guidance)

INITIATE

Good hosts take initiative with their guests. They greet them at the door, offer to take their jackets, and start up conversations. As a result, their guests feel welcomed and become responsive. Good hosts make others feel like the most important person in the room. It works the same way in daily relationships. When we make the first move, others tend to let down their guard and engage with us. But it takes initiative on our part to get the ball rolling. Leaders go first.

Sometimes we fail to host by saying, "Well, I'm the leader. They can come to me." Other times we may fail to host others because our "antennas" simply aren't up. We become so caught up in the busyness of life that we neglect those around us. JoAnn Jones discovered this one day when her professor asked the class an unexpected question. She writes,

> During my second month of nursing school, our professor gave us a pop quiz. I was a conscientious student and had breezed through the questions, until I read the last one: "What is the first name of the woman who cleans the school?" Surely this was some kind of joke. I had seen the cleaning woman several times. She was tall, dark-haired, and in her 50s, but how would I know her name? I handed in my paper, leaving the last question blank. Before class ended, one student asked if the last question would count towards our grade. "Absolutely," said the professor. "In your careers you will meet many people. All are significant. They deserve your attention and care, even if all you do is smile and say hello." I've never forgotten that lesson. I also learned that her name was Dorothy.[1]

Connect

Good hosts connect with their guests. They do their best to help them feel comfortable and at ease. They're always trying to find common ground with others. Instead of dominating conversations, they focus on others and let them be the main attraction. Leaders have a similar mindset. They know it's not about them—it's about creating an environment for others to feel at home with them.

The Walt Disney Company seems to have an intrinsic understanding of how important this is. Everything it does is centered on creating happy experiences for others, especially children. In fact, they refer to all their customers as "guests" and treat them accordingly. I have a friend who works in the Imagineering department. He once told me that Disney employees are always expected to go above and beyond the basics when "hosting" others. For example, if a child drops her lollipop on the ground and begins to cry, any employee is authorized to run to the nearest gift shop and buy her a new one on the spot, with the company picking up the bill! Disney understands the importance of connecting with others. When they say, "Be our guest," they really mean it!

Connecting with others is important, but let's be honest, it's not always easy. As you strive to be a better host, you're bound to run across some people who are very different from you. You'll find yourself saying things like, "I've tried to be friends with her, but we just don't have anything in common." Or, "We always end up arguing. He's just not worth the effort!"

It can be tempting to throw in the towel. Don't. Instead, try using the 101% Principle: find the 1% that you have in common with someone, and devote 100% of your attention to it. Maybe you both enjoy tennis, like the same music, or love the same sports team. Whatever it is, find it and zero in on it. It may take some effort to discover that 1%, but you'll be glad you did in the end.

Provide

Good hosts provide for their guests. They prepare delicious meals, plan engaging activities, and anticipate needs that may arise. As a result, their guests become satisfied and look forward to a return visit. Leaders play a similar role. They meet the needs of those around them and look for ways to benefit them.

When we start looking, it's amazing how many needs there are around us. When we start leading, it's amazing how many of those needs we can meet. One of the great needs today is relational leadership. People today are crying out for relational leaders—leaders who connect with their hearts, not just their heads. It's no longer enough just to be competent or have strong character. To lead effectively, you'll need to have strong people skills as well. That's what this little book is all about.

One of the most basic ways we can provide relational leadership is by adding value to others. By "adding value," I mean improving someone else's life by sharing your own. I've made a goal to do this with every single person I come in contact with for more than ten minutes. It can happen in a variety of ways. Sometimes I'll tell a story from my own experience and the light bulb will come on for someone else. Other times I'll share a book, an encouraging word, or help someone through a personal crisis. However it happens, my goal is for others to be better off after having spent time with me. It's my way of providing for them.

A friend once told me, "I don't remember what someone does or how well they did it; I remember how they made me feel." What a great line for us to remember. We don't need to be perfect, but we do need to show others that we care.

DIRECT

Good hosts give direction to their guests. They help them know when the party starts, the location, how to get there, and what to expect once they arrive. They don't make others figure it out on their own. As a result, their guests receive guidance. Leaders direct others as well. They know that others are looking to them for clarity on which way to go.

Beyond simply telling others what to do, leaders provide direction in the following ways:

- Suggesting a variety of options for those facing a dilemma.

- Giving resources and instruction based on past experience.

- Helping others do a "self-discovery" to guide them along the way.

- Placing others in contact with key people to help them on their journey.

Years ago, I decided I was going to be a host, not a guest, in the relationships of my life. This is a challenge for me because I am a natural introvert. I am tempted to be passive in relationships and let others take the first step. Even with my family, instead of vegging in front of the TV watching ESPN, I try to host my wife and kids. A few years ago, I surprised my wife with a Valentine's weekend in Paris, France. (I got a great deal on tickets!) We toured museums, ate crepes, soared to the top of the Eiffel Tower, and laughed a ton. It was an unforgettable weekend. On the flight home, I asked my wife what her favorite part of the trip was. After reflecting for a moment, she smiled and said, "I think it was simply that you took the initiative on everything from the travel, to the hotel, to the babysitting responsibilities. You were the host. You were the leader." Hmmm. That's when it hit me that maybe hosting and leading go together.

REFLECT AND RESPOND

Good hosts are always looking for ways to connect with their guests. They initiate the conversation, create a comfortable environment, and ask questions to find a common interest.

1. At parties, most people view themselves as "guests." In our relationships, why is it that the majority of us expect others to make the first move?

_____

_____

_____

_____

2. What motivates leaders to take the initiative and be a host? How are leaders different from others in this respect?

_____

_____

_____

_____

3. What effect does a bad attitude have on being a good host? What kind of attitude do hosts need?

_____

_____

_____

_____

Self-Assessment

Think about your daily interactions with others—at work, in school, while doing errands, etc. Are you a host or a guest? Go through the following chart and indicate where you fall on the scale.

Hosts	USUALLY	SOMETIMES	USUALLY	Guests
Make the phone call	←		→	Wait for the phone call
Introduce themselves	←		→	Are introduced by others
Focus on similarities	←		→	Focus on differences
Put others at ease	←		→	Put others on edge
Look to serve	←		→	Look to be served
Add value to others	←		→	Add nothing to others
Offer clear advice	←		→	Need clear advice
Proactive; take initiative	←		→	Reactive; passive

Over the years, I've noticed that there are four main obstacles that keep people from becoming good hosts. Evaluate yourself. Do you relate to any of the obstacles? Discuss your thoughts

1. FEAR
   "What will they think of me? What if I say something stupid?"

2. PRIDE
   "Don't they know who I am? They should come to me."

3. LAZINESS
   "It's too much work… I'd rather not make the effort."

4. PERSONALITY
   "I'm not naturally outgoing, so why even try?"

Take a moment to do an honest evaluation on being a good host or hostess in your relationships. Assess yourself in the following four areas:

1. INITIATE
   How do others respond to you?

   < POOR 1 2 3 4 5 6 7 8 9 10 EXCELLENT >

2. CONNECT
   How comfortable are people around you?

   < POOR 1 2 3 4 5 6 7 8 9 10 EXCELLENT >

3. PROVIDE
   Do your guests feel satisfied?

   < POOR 1 2 3 4 5 6 7 8 9 10 EXCELLENT >

4. DIRECT
   How well do others receive guidance from you?

   < POOR 1 2 3 4 5 6 7 8 9 10 EXCELLENT >

EXERCISE

Host a meal at your house (or dorm room), but instead of inviting your close friends, invite some people whom you've just met or don't know very well. This will challenge you to get out of your comfort zone and initiate contact with others. During the evening, try to be deliberate about applying the principles you've learned in this chapter. (Remember, the goal is not to dominate but to direct; not to control but to connect.) After everyone leaves, spend time reflecting. Were you a good host? Did you connect? What did you learn about yourself?

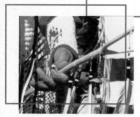

The Indian Talking Stick

THE INDIAN TALKING STICK REMINDS US THAT BEFORE WE LEAD, WE MUST LISTEN. LEADERS SEEK TO UNDERSTAND THE PERSPECTIVES OF OTHERS BEFORE THEY COMMUNICATE THEIR OWN POINTS. THEY SHOW EMPATHY AND ASK GOOD QUESTIONS. AS A RESULT, THEY EARN THE RIGHT TO BE HEARD.

The atmosphere is tense. Conflict is in the air. The two tribes have been known to disagree before, but recent events have led many to believe that war is on the horizon. As the council members assemble, the two chiefs join the circle, both facing each other without saying a word. For several moments there is only silence… Then, in a burst of emotion, the group erupts with angry shouts and accusations. No one is listening, and it looks like violence is inevitable. That is, until the visiting chief steps forward and raises the Talking Stick. Suddenly, the atmosphere begins to change…

It's been around for centuries, yet few have ever heard of it. Here's how it works. During the meeting, the Indian Talking Stick is passed around from person to person, but only the one holding it is allowed to speak. It remains in the speaker's possession until he/she feels completely understood by everyone in the group. The only exception is when the speaker might lend it to someone who is seeking to clarify the speaker's point. Once the point is clarified, the stick returns to the speaker until he believes he is fully understood. Only then is it passed to the next individual.

It's a simple concept, but the end result is quite remarkable. As the tribal members pass the stick around, they slowly become less combative and more cohesive. Each person feels like his or her view is getting a fair hearing. Before long, the real source of the conflict is revealed, and new solutions begin forming. War is averted. Relationships are restored. All because the focus is on understanding, not just being understood.

Without question, the greatest emotional need of people today is the need to be understood. And to understand, we must listen. Leaders *have* to get this. If they don't, it doesn't matter how intelligent, gifted, or charismatic they are. They will ultimately fail to connect with others and end up sabotaging their true potential.

But it's not easy; most of us aren't naturally good at listening (myself included). We have to work at it, being diligent and alert to the needs around us. Case in point: did you know that when the Titanic was sinking, a ship was just thirty miles away that could have come to the rescue? Unfortunately, it never heard the distress call. The radio operator on board had just gone to bed. If he had only listened a little while longer, he would have heard the SOS and turned the ship around. Instead, his ship continued on its way, oblivious to the tragedy unfolding around it.

When it comes to listening, leaders simply cannot afford to fall asleep on the job. Often, as much as 50% of leadership is about listening, observing, and interpreting what we see and hear. So how do we learn to do this well? How do we practice the Indian Talking Stick in our everyday lives?

Poor Listening Habits

To start with, we've got to identify the bad listening habits we may have picked up over the years:

- *Judgmental listening* – jumping to conclusions about the speaker.

- *Selective listening* – only hearing what you want to hear.

- *Impatient listening* – finishing other people's sentences, interrupting them.

- *Egocentric listening* – thinking about what you'll say as others are talking.

- *Patronizing listening* – pretending to listen, but really off in your own world.

- *Stubborn listening* – listening, but not open—your mind is already made up.

Can you relate to any of these common pitfalls? Your ability to move past them will have a profound impact on your leadership… and your daily interactions with others.

Many leaders never learn to listen well. They're so focused on their own agendas that they tune out everyone else. The results can be tragic. Robert McNamara confirms this in his book, *In Retrospect*.[1] As the U.S. entered the Vietnam War, numerous CIA agents warned top White House officials that failure was inevitable. All the data indicated that the North Vietnamese were a new type of enemy and that a conventional bombing campaign would not work. But their warnings were ignored. By the time the war was over, over 58,000 U.S. soldiers were either dead or missing in action and little military progress had been made. All because a group of leaders failed to listen.

Learning to Listen

If you want to become a great listener, you'll need to work on two things: showing empathy and asking good questions. Allow me to explain.

Show Empathy

Empathy is about entering into another person's situation. It involves understanding how others feel and showing that you genuinely care. Counselors are usually great at this. You'll see them nod, show concern in their faces, give an occasional "hmmm," and display real interest in what you're saying. When they listen, you feel understood and your emotions are validated. And here's the kicker: when they finally do speak up, you're all ears. Why? Their ability to listen has earned them the right to be heard. It's the same with us. When we listen empathetically to others, they tend to become receptive to what we have to say in return. They see that we're not focused on advancing our agenda or "winning" the conversation.

I recently met a missionary who worked in Africa for two years without seeing any results. Despite the fact that he was well trained and had earned three doctorates, he couldn't seem to connect with the people there. Week after week his church remained empty. When his son died tragically, he found a local man to help him with the burial. Overwhelmed by grief, the missionary slumped over the casket and began to weep. He sobbed for several minutes. Watching intently, the African man grabbed his hair, picked up his head, and looked him in the eyes. Then, he gently set the missionary's head back down on the pine box, and ran back to the village. He told everyone, "The white man cries like we do." The next Sunday the missionary's church was full.

Why? The people didn't want a leader who impressed them. They were interested in a leader who identified with them. Others want to see that you're human, not a walking encyclopedia. It's an old cliché, but it's true: "People don't care how much you know until they know how much you care." Do the people you lead know how much you care about them? Do they share openly with you?

Ask Good Questions

Showing empathy is important, but so is asking relevant questions. Stop for a second and recall the last time you visited the doctor's office. Did the doctor just barge through the door and immediately begin trying to sell you the latest and greatest drug on the market? I sure hope not! Any doctor worth her salt knows that you never give a prescription without first making a diagnosis. Doctors take the time to look into your eyes, listen to your heartbeat, ask where it hurts, etc. Only after poking and prodding will they draw a conclusion and give you a prescription.

Let me ask you a question. Have you learned to poke and prod during your conversations with others? Or, do you make assumptions and jump to conclusions? How you answer says a lot about your listening ability. Many leaders are guilty of jamming stuff down people's throats because they believe they're supposed to have answers, not questions. They never ask, afraid they'll appear weak. But asking good questions doesn't make you weak; well-placed questions help you connect with people and understand where they're really coming from. It's a sign of strength.

Making Deposits and Withdrawals

Over the years I've come to realize that great listening is a little like banking. You have to make deposits before you can make withdrawals. It would be silly to walk up to a bank teller and request money if you had never started an account and put money in it! It's the same way with people. We've got to make relational deposits into others' lives before they'll listen to us.

I remember this truth through a little acronym, SALT:

* S – Say anything

* A – Ask questions

* L – Listen well

* T – Turn the topic in a positive direction

I remember sitting next to a sharp professional woman on a flight some time ago. She was dressed formally, carried a leather briefcase, and seemed to have more money than she knew what to do with. I initiated the conversation with something light and easy. (The point is to say something—anything—just to get the ball rolling.) Then, I began to ask questions. We talked about her thriving career, her car, and her summer house in the Rocky Mountains. She talked for nearly two hours. My job was to listen. I began to think she had her act completely together. Finally, I asked her about her family. She stopped smiling and looked downward at the floor. I knew I had hit a sensitive issue, so I remained silent to allow her to collect her thoughts. When she looked up, tears had filled her eyes. She began sharing that she was going through a divorce, and she wasn't sure if she or her husband were going to get custody of their two children. She paused. I recognized it was finally my turn to respond to her. I gently said, "I am so sorry you are going through this tough time. I wish I could say I understand—but I can't. I've never been divorced. However, I do have a listening ear, and if you want to talk to someone about it, I'll be glad to listen." The Indian Talking Stick reminds leaders that if they want to connect with others, they must first learn how to listen. This Habitude can revolutionize your day-to-day life. Your relationships will be strengthened and your influence will increase. It all begins with showing empathy and asking good questions. Practice these two and you'll be on your way in connecting with others.

Reflect and Respond

There is a progression that takes place before a leader earns the right to be heard. First, we must learn how to listen. Leaders must focus on understanding others' viewpoints before they can expect to be understood.

1. What is the greatest emotional need of people today? In what ways did the Indian Talking Stick change the atmosphere between the two hostile Indian tribes?

_____

_____

_____

_____

2. Why do you think we are more inclined to talk than to listen? What is your biggest hindrance to being a good listener?

_____

_____

_____

_____

3. Connecting with others begins with showing empathy and asking good questions. In the context of being a good listener, describe some ways you can show empathy.

_____

_____

_____

_____

4. Explain how being a good listener is like going to the bank. Using the acronym, SALT, what four steps remind you how to engage someone in a conversation?

_____

_____

_____

_____

5. Asking questions is sometimes associated with appearing weak. After reading this chapter, what would be your response to that assumption?

_____

_____

_____

_____

Getting Personal

Think about your own listening ability. On a scale of one to ten, how would you rate yourself as a listener? If you're really brave, have a friend fill it out for you!

1. I display empathy and show genuine interest in others.

   < POOR 1 2 3 4 5 6 7 8 9 10 EXCELLENT >

2. My body language shows attentiveness.

   < POOR 1 2 3 4 5 6 7 8 9 10 EXCELLENT >

3. I seek to understand before being understood.

   < POOR 1 2 3 4 5 6 7 8 9 10 EXCELLENT >

4. I ask relevant questions and engage in others' thoughts.

   < POOR 1 2 3 4 5 6 7 8 9 10 EXCELLENT >

5. I am open; I avoid judging others or interrupting them.

   < POOR 1 2 3 4 5 6 7 8 9 10 EXCELLENT >

Exercise

College student Brett Banfe made headlines when he announced that he was going to stop talking for an entire year. Some wondered if it was just a publicity stunt. Others doubted it was even possible. But Brett came through in the end. Not only did he meet his goal, he went a step further and posted a journal about what he was learning through the experience. When asked why he would attempt such a feat, Brett responded, "I'm embarrassed to say… that I wouldn't listen to people when they talked. I'd wait for them to stop talking, then I'd start. Because… my opinion was the right one anyway. I was like 'Thanks for your input, but here's how it really [is].'"

My challenge to you: try going just one day without speaking. For some of you this will seem like torture! It won't be easy, but give it your best shot. Focus all your energy on listening well. Carry a notepad with you and write down your observations. What was the most challenging part? Why? What did you learn about yourself? Share your notes with a friend on the following day.

IMAGE THREE
[Chess and Checkers]

Chess and Checkers

IN CHECKERS, ALL THE GAME PIECES MOVE IN THE SAME WAY. IN CHESS, YOU MOVE
EACH PIECE DIFFERENTLY BASED ON ITS ABILITY. WISE LEADERS PLAY CHESS, NOT
CHECKERS, AS THEY MANAGE RELATIONSHIPS. THEY CONNECT WITH INDIVIDUALS
BASED ON THEIR UNIQUE PERSONALITIES AND STRENGTHS.

Growing up, I loved to play checkers. I had three versions of the game at my house
and would play my grandpa, my friends, my sisters, or my parents any time they
were willing. I got pretty good at it. By fifth grade, I was introduced to the game
of chess. Wow. I had no idea that two games played on the same board could be
so different. All of a sudden I entered a whole new world of strategy. Think about
it. What is the biggest difference between checkers and chess? It's the pieces.
Anyone who wants to win in chess has to first learn how each piece moves—from
the pawn, to the rook, to the knight, to the queen and king. Once I understood the
ability of each chess piece, I could plan a strategy to win the game. Bobby Fischer,
the great chess champion, once said, "Winning in this game is all a matter of
understanding how to capitalize on the strengths of each piece and timing their
moves just right."

This is a picture of good leadership. Great managers understand that you can't get
the best out of people by playing "checkers" with them—treating them all alike,
expecting the same things out of each of them, handling them like some generic
product on a shelf. Just like in chess, great managers discover what is unique about
each person and capitalize on it. Marcus Buckingham inspired this Habitude.[1] He
notes how employees will differ in how they think, how they build relationships,
how they learn, how prepared they need to feel, what drives them, and so on. (Most
of these differences don't change.) The best way to connect with people is to
identify how each one is different and how you can best incorporate those differences
into your plan of action. Great managing is not about control, but about connection
and release. It's not about your power but your empowerment of others. And folks
are best empowered when it is done according to their strengths. Mediocre managers
play checkers with their people. Excellent managers play chess. They connect with
people at the point of their strengths.

Michael Abrashoff once served as the executive officer aboard the Navy ship, *U.S.S. Shiloh*. It was a dreaded job because, in addition to being second in command, he was in charge of the entire bureaucracy of paperwork for 440 sailors. His administrative assistant was a man who got promoted only because he'd been around longer than anyone else. He could not type, proofread, or use the spellchecker; and what he did do—he did extremely slowly.

At first, Mike assumed he had to endure this inevitable situation. One day, however, his assistant went on vacation, leaving him adrift in a sea of paper. Since his job was so unpleasant, Mike grabbed a junior seaman named David, who'd been transferred because he didn't fit in anywhere and who'd been charged with insubordination. Needless to say, Mike didn't expect much from him. Soon after David arrived, however, the piles of paper were finding homes. Stacks were disappearing, words were being spelled correctly, and sentences actually had subjects and verbs for the first time!

One day, Mike asked David why he'd been kicked out of his last post. Mike replied, "I felt as though the chief petty officer hated me." He then explained that a month after arriving there he began suggesting ways to improve their efficiency and the chief didn't like it. He hit a brick wall over and over again. Eventually, David gave up. In reality, David was simply demonstrating his strengths, and that officer didn't know how to handle it. He only knew the world that promotes people based on tenure not talent; based on rank and not strength. He only knew how to play checkers—not chess. Needless to say, David flourished under Mike's leadership because he allowed David to think freely and create ways to improve what they did. He invited David to draft letters and decide the best way to solve problems in his strength area. Mike turned out to be quite a chess player.[2]

If you followed professional football in the 1990s, you know the name Bo Jackson. Bo was an all-pro running back in the NFL for years. But did you know we may have never heard of Bo Jackson had it not been for his coach at Auburn University? You see, Bo Jackson began as a defensive player for Auburn. As fate would have it, the two starting players in the backfield at Auburn both got hurt at about the same time. His coach approached Bo and asked him to play tailback. Bo hesitated—but said yes. And the rest is history. He may be the best tailback Auburn has ever graduated. He went on to win the Heisman Trophy.

So what am I saying? Bo was good at his defensive position, but he was great at his offensive position. He simply needed to be placed well. He needed a coach who could spot potential talent outside of the box he'd been placed inside. Bo needed a leader who played chess, not checkers.

How to Play Chess as a Leader

In order to play chess, you must recognize the unique role each player on the team can fill. This means we must identify at least four qualities in others:

1. **STRENGTHS AND WEAKNESSES** – Leaders must connect with people at the point of their strengths. We must identify both the weaknesses that de-energize them and waste time as well as strong points where they get energized, have natural intuition and flourish.

2. **TRIGGERS** – Leaders must figure out what motivates their team members. Is it verbal praise? Is it time with the leader? Is it monetary gifts? Everybody has a trigger that gets them motivated and ready to give themselves to the cause.

3. **PERSONALITY** – It's key for leaders to know the personality differences of their people. Are they the fun-loving sanguine? Or the driven choleric? Or the laid-back phlegmatic? Or the analytical melancholy? Identifying personalities can make or break your leadership.

4. **LEARNING STYLE** – Finally, leaders must discover their people's learning styles. Is he an "analyzer" who craves information? Is she the "doer" who has to actually jump in and do it? Or are they "watchers" who want to see it modeled in order to learn something?

Capitalizing on each person's strengths accomplishes so many things for a leader. First, it saves you time. You don't waste time anymore trying to change people. Second, it makes others accountable. Each person is encouraged to do his or her very best in an area. Third, it builds a stronger sense of team, since the best teams are built around interdependency. You acknowledge you need others because they do things you can't do. You can celebrate differences. Others' value is in their differences. (A baseball team doesn't need four shortstops!) Think about it: a mediocre leader believes value must be taught. An excellent leader believes that the best is already inside of people—they just need to find it. So, while a mediocre leader's goal is to overcome weaknesses; the excellent leader's goal is to identify strength and focus on it.

REFLECT AND RESPOND

The best way for a leader to build an effective team is to identify how each one is different and how to successfully incorporate those differences into the overall plan of action. The strength that each person possesses meets a certain need on the team. Great managing is not about control, but about connection and release.

1. Explain what this phrase means. "Great managers understand you can't get the best out of people by playing 'checkers' with them."

_____

_____

_____

_____

_____

2. Why is it we naturally expect others to be like us? Why are we more comfortable with people who are similar to us?

_____

_____

_____

_____

3. What are the four qualities that leaders must identify in each team member in order to play "chess" instead of "checkers?"

_____

_____

_____

_____

4. Describe the benefits of learning how to capitalize on each person's strengths.

_____

_____

_____

_____

Self-Assessment

Evaluate how well you connect with people based on their unique strengths. Besides giving them personality tests and learning style assessments, try observing your group and asking yourself:

1. Do I understand the personality of each member? Do I see how they work best together?

2. Do I know what motivates each one of them?

3. Do I recognize the primary strength the individual brings to the group or team?

4. Do I realize how they best learn something new?

Exercise

Meet with your group and ask them these questions. Tell them it will help you play "chess" better...

1. For Strengths:
   What was the best day at your job this past year? Or, describe your perfect job. What is it you'd really like to do and feel you would do well?

2. For Triggers:
   What was the best relationship you ever had with a manager or teacher? What made that person so motivating? What was the best praise you ever received?

3. For Personality:
   When you work on a project with a team, what do you like best: Getting results? Just being together? Doing the project with excellence? Having fun?

4. For Style of Learning:
   In your past jobs, when did you feel you were learning the most? Why did you learn so much? What's the best way for you to learn?

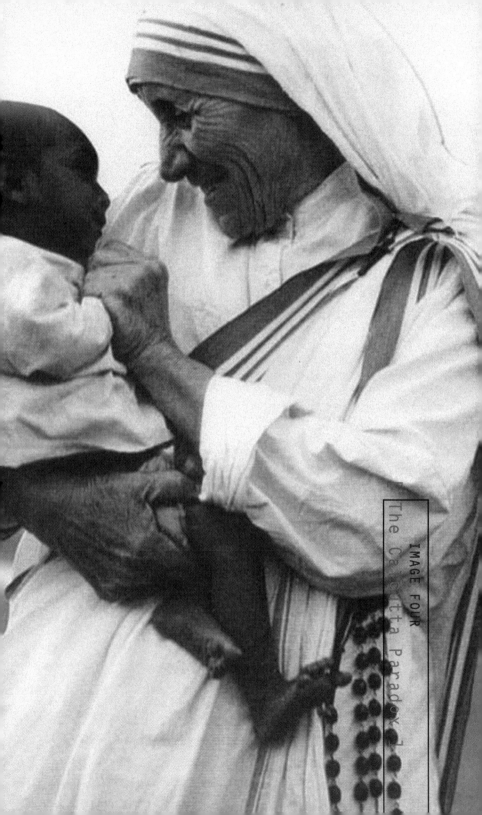

IMAGE FOUR   The Calcutta Paradox

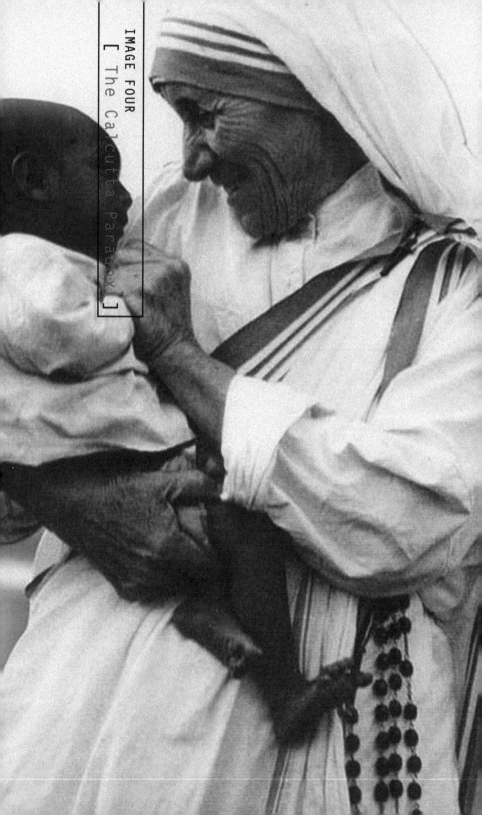

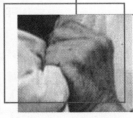

The Calcutta Paradox

HUMILITY IS MAGNETIC IN A LEADER. WHEN WE "UNDER-SPEAK" WITH REGARD TO OUR VALUE, OTHERS ARE DRAWN TOWARD US AND OUR INFLUENCE INCREASES. WHEN WE "OVER-SPEAK," OTHERS ARE REPELLED. WHEN IT COMES TO SELF-DESCRIPTION, LEADERS KNOW PEOPLE WILL FILL WHAT IS LACKING AND EMPTY WHAT IS TOO FULL.

In 1997, I was part of a team who was invited to come and teach leadership in India. One of the highlights would be a special meeting with Mother Teresa in Calcutta. Unfortunately, she died in August, just three months before we arrived. Ugh. Although it was one of my dreams, I never did get to meet that great, little woman.

We did, however, visit her headquarters, the Missionaries of Charity. It was tucked back into an alley, away from the main street. I was struck by how simple it was. There were Sisters, all on the floor, serving lepers, or wiping the sores from children's arms and legs or feeding homeless men. That's it. No neon lights. No flashy websites advertised. No plush toys to buy as souvenirs. We could tell the leadership Mother Teresa modeled for fifty years was simple and humble.

Maybe that's what made her so attractive to the world. She led, but she never called attention to herself. I discovered on the trip that Mother Teresa entered the world of the poor on August 17, 1948. She started alone, with no funding from St. Mary's High School where she'd been the principal. She left the famous, comfortable, elite school which served rich families to go to a slum where people lived in misery among rats and cockroaches, teaching the children of the nobodies… and serving anyone who needed help. She remembers, "One day, in a heap of rubbish I found a woman who was half dead. Her body had been bitten by rats and ants. I took her to a hospital, but they told me that they didn't want her because they couldn't do anything for her. I protested and said I wouldn't leave unless they hospitalized her. They had a long meeting and finally granted my request. That woman was saved. Afterwards, when thanking me for what I had done for her, she said, 'and to think it was my son who threw me into the garbage.'"[1]

Mother Teresa felt she'd passed from heaven to hell. But she did it on purpose. When asked why she moved to the slums, she replied: "How can I serve the poor effectively unless I understand what they experience each day?" One by one, her former students at the high school began to join her. It grew over the years to become the largest order of its kind, with locations worldwide. She launched or inspired seven other organizations for both men and women, clergy and laypeople, to be involved. She won a Nobel Peace Prize in 1979. She spoke at Harvard's graduation. She spoke to presidents, and for several years she was voted the most influential woman in the world.

It's an amazing story. But what enabled Mother Teresa to attract so many people? I call it the Calcutta Paradox. It was the fact that she was humble and didn't like attention—that magnetically drew others to her. It was the fact that she didn't pursue fame that made her famous. It was the fact that she downplayed her importance—that made her so irreplaceable as a leader. Several times she was asked about the secret to her work. She would only smile and sheepishly say, "I am just a little pencil in the hand of a writing God who is sending a love letter to the world."

Think about this principle. Have you ever heard someone ask an outstanding leader about her work or about the book she recently wrote—and that leader humbly brushed it off as nothing spectacular? How do listeners who know the truth respond? It makes them want to talk about how great that leader is or how great that book is. Why? Because the leader didn't do it. People tend to fill what is lacking in a leader's description of himself, and empty what is too full. It's the Calcutta Paradox. When we brush fame aside, when we downplay our accomplishments, it is actually winsome and magnetic to people. They will start talking. People tend to over-speak about the leader who will only under-speak.

This principle shows up in all sorts of contexts. A few months ago, our organization, Growing Leaders, hosted a Leadership Forum for college deans. During the Forum, one dean, Mike, commented that his top student attended our leadership camp (Converge Atlanta) the previous May. He raved about how that student's life had been transformed. He went on and on about it. Hearing him talk deliriously about it, one of our team members asked him to share a testimony after the next session. That, however, is when we saw the Calcutta Paradox work in reverse. While introducing Mike, our team member began to talk about how this student's life had been incredibly transformed by our leadership camp. He didn't say anything that Mike hadn't already said, but he stole Mike's thunder. Our team member unwittingly took the "rave" out of this dean. After the long introduction, Mike stood up and under-spoke about his student. Ouch. It totally ruined the moment. Why? Because we had over-spoken. This caused him to want to balance the comments so as not to distort them. Our team member should have humbly introduced him by saying, "We'd like to introduce a dean to you whose student attended our leadership camp. He mentioned it had a somewhat positive effect on him. Would you share about your student, Mike?" Can you guess what kind of testimonial that dean might have given? He would have raved again, because we under-spoke. Remember: people fill what is lacking and they empty what is too full.

Many of the greatest leaders in history—the ones we yearn to be like—are humble leaders. Why? The Calcutta Paradox. We're drawn to humility. Billy Graham won over the skeptical press when he first visited England in 1954. Those reporters mocked him at the beginning of his crusades there in Britain, yet by the end—they were praising him. And it wasn't his flashy preaching that changed them. It was his humility. In Jim Collins' book, *Good to Great*, he talks about Level Five Leaders: those who reached the top; leaders who took their company from being "good" to being "great." His research team was shocked by what they found in these leaders. He said he expected those companies to be led by charismatic leaders, with huge personalities and even bigger egos. Instead, he found the opposite. They were leaders with "windows and mirrors." When something went right, they looked out the window and said: "Look at this team. Look at what they achieved." When something went wrong, they looked in the mirror and said: "How can I improve to lead this team better?"[2]

Several years ago, I led a chapel meeting before a ballgame between the San Diego Padres and the Chicago Cubs. Ryne Sandberg was an all-star second baseman for the Chicago Cubs at the time. And he got paid very well for his skills. Unfortunately, that year Ryne was in a hitting slump and wasn't playing near his potential. We talked after the chapel, and he confessed to me it really hurt him to be performing so poorly but being paid so well. He also told me it angered the fans in Chicago. Fans and reporters criticized him for being this highly paid athlete who didn't meet the standard. And the ball club wasn't happy either. It was a difficult time for everyone. Several weeks later, however, I remember reading how Ryne decided to handle his situation. In addition to improving his swing, he met with the general manager of the Cubs and offered a large chunk of his salary back to the team. Yes, you read that right. He told them he didn't feel right about taking millions of dollars when he wasn't performing up to his potential. He wanted to give some money back. Wow. Needless to say, Ryne won the fans over by this act. Those who had booed him were now praising him… even before he got his good swing back. Why? The Calcutta Paradox. He assumed the humble position and won their hearts. They were magnetically drawn to him.

Humility doesn't mean weakness. These kinds of leaders are strong—but they're secure enough to see beyond themselves. They're not worried about their images. They know their value, but it isn't about them. It's about a cause much bigger than them. Humility doesn't mean leaders think less of themselves. It means they think of themselves less. And this… makes others think more of them.

Reflect and Respond

In spite of the fact that Mother Teresa never called attention to herself, nor did she portray the glamour that Hollywood applauds, people around the globe found her humility very attractive. It's a paradox that for 50 years she served in the slums of Calcutta, yet she was voted the most influential woman in the world… for several years. People tend to over-speak about leaders who will only under-speak about themselves.

1. Why do some people tend to insist on taking places of honor or seeking words of honor for themselves?

_____

_____

_____

_____

_____

2. Why is it that leaders who humbly "under-speak" about themselves are so attractive?

_____

_____

_____

_____

_____

3. What leaders do you admire for their humility? How would you respond to those who say that humility indicates weakness?

_____

_____

_____

_____

_____

4. If you know of any leaders that operate with the "windows and mirrors" leadership style, describe the effect it has on their team.

_____

_____

_____

_____

_____

Self-Assessment

As weird as it seems, people are magnetically drawn to leaders who are humble. These leaders aren't weak. They are secure, and they can see beyond themselves. When leaders think of themselves *less*, it makes others think *more* of them. Now, assess how well you practice this principle of humility.

1. From where do you receive your sense of identity?

_____

_____

_____

_____

_____

2. How often do you attempt to project an image that appears to have it all together?

_____

_____

_____

_____

_____

3. Do you regularly depend upon your own strength and wisdom instead of asking for wise counsel from others?

_____

_____

_____

_____

_____

4. Are you able to publicly acknowledge your weaknesses and your need for the team?

_____

_____

_____

_____

_____

EXERCISE

This week, attempt three acts of kindness—anonymously. Don't let anyone know what you're up to, including the ones who will receive the act of kindness. It may be as simple as sending them an encouraging email or mailing them a handwritten note. Or, it could be as creative as restocking the fridge with their favorite soft drink. After you perform these acts of kindnesses, examine your heart. It's a motive check. How did this make you feel? Are you okay with serving without getting any credit? Journal your thoughts and feelings.

During this same week, practice The Calcutta Paradox. Under-speak any good deeds you may do, and express humility whenever one of your accomplishments comes up in a conversation. Don't deny the praise of others; thank them for it, but don't play into it. See what it does to your heart. See what it does to others. Do they find it attractive? Write down what happens.

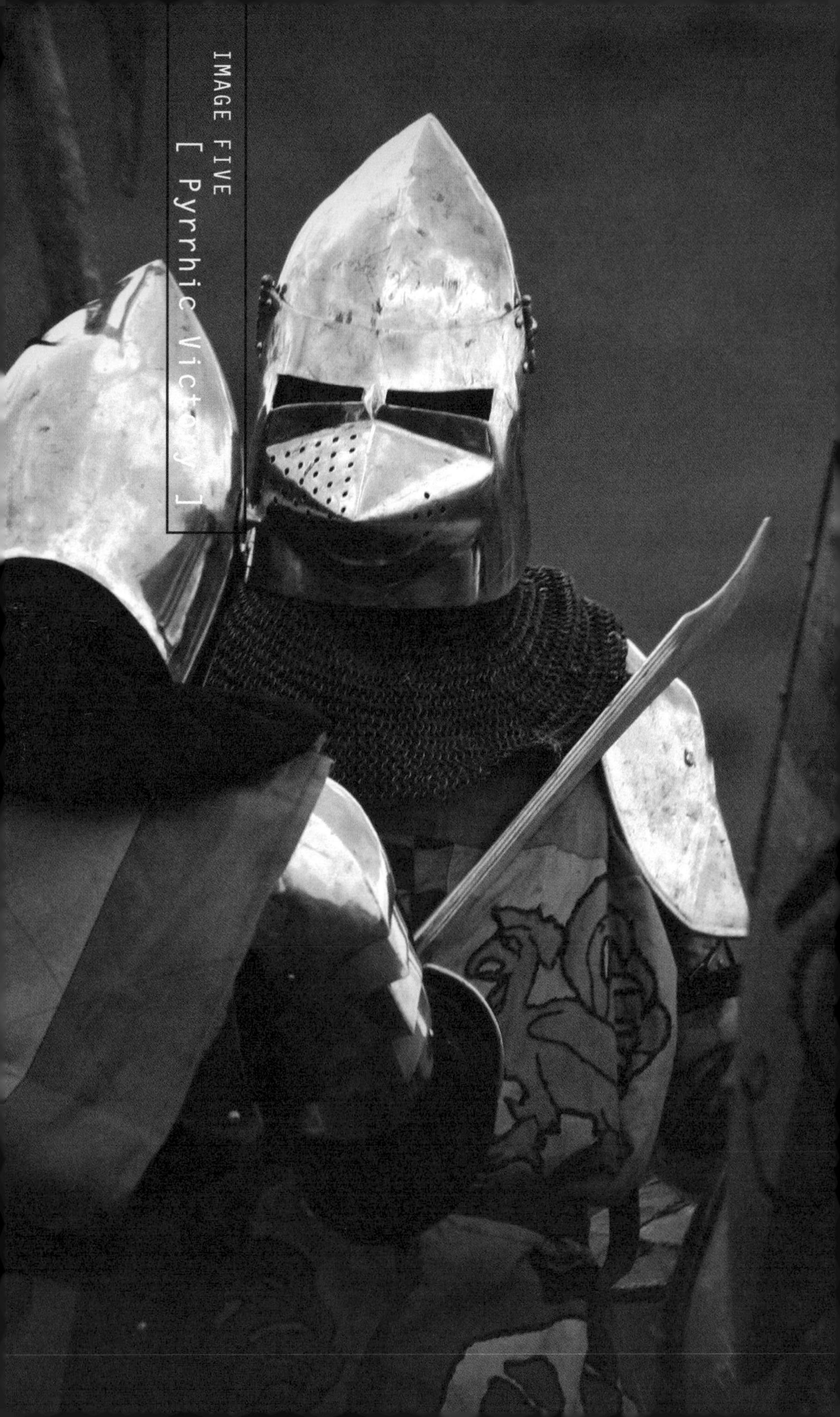

IMAGE FIVE
[Pyrrhic Victory]

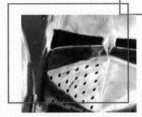

Pyrrhic Victory

SOMETIMES THE COST OF WINNING IS SO GREAT THAT WE LOSE MORE THAN WE
GAIN. GOOD LEADERS DON'T FIGHT EVERY BATTLE. THEY CAREFULLY CONSIDER
WHAT'S AT STAKE IN EACH ENCOUNTER WITH OTHERS AND THEN ACT
ACCORDINGLY. THEY NEVER ALLOW THE SITUATION TO BECOME MORE IMPORTANT
THAN THE RELATIONSHIP.

The battle lines were drawn—40,000 Greeks versus 40,000 Romans. King Pyrrhus had
his sights set on Rome, and no one was going to stand in his way. He'd brought cavalry,
archers, and even war elephants with him. His track record was nearly flawless. Surely
the Roman Empire would fall. But after several days of fierce combat, it still wasn't clear
who would win. Both sides had suffered major casualties, and it looked like a stalemate.

Then, at last, the Greeks managed to prevail. Their elephants broke through the enemy
line, the Romans were driven back, and Pyrrhus won his battle. Unfortunately, his army
was now incredibly weak. He was far from home and couldn't gather reinforcements
quickly. The enemy could. When a friend congratulated him on his win, Pyrrhus
responded "One more such victory and I am lost." He never did conquer Rome.

Some battles are won at too great a cost. They end up hurting us more than helping
us. They're Pyrrhic Victories. Like King Pyrrhus, we often want to win so badly that
we end up defeating ourselves. We lose more than we gain. One of the big ways this
plays itself out is in interpersonal relationships. Think about it. We've all been
involved in some pretty ugly arguments. We fight so hard to win that we end up
steamrolling right over others. We win the fight but lose the friendship.

Todd is a friend of mine. He recently told me of a phone conversation he had with
a client at work. They had a misunderstanding about when a product was to be
delivered to his customer. The phone call turned into a major disagreement. Todd is
pretty good at arguing, so he was determined to convince everyone it wasn't his fault.
After building his case, and outsmarting his client, the client said, "Okay, Todd. You
win." And she hung up the phone. Todd felt good about his victory, until he realized
later—that customer wouldn't do business with him anymore. Ouch. He won the
argument, but it was a Pyrrhic Victory. He allowed the situation to become more

important than the relationship. I have done the same thing. During the 1980s, I worked with college students in San Diego. Two of my interns got into a squabble over some petty issue, and I failed to resolve the problem as their leader. Finally, when I got involved, my pride was so great that I wasn't able to apologize right away; I felt I had to defend myself. The result? Several students left the organization because of my poor leadership. I had protected my pride—but lost many relationships.

If only Todd and I had both stopped to count the cost before the conflict—a lot of hurt could have been avoided and some relationships could have been salvaged. I've learned that just because I can win, doesn't mean I should. Some battles simply aren't worth fighting. It takes discernment to determine which ones to begin.

When you're on the verge of entering into a heated argument or conflict with someone else, sometimes it's good to pause and ask yourself a few key questions:

- Is this issue worth debating?
- What do I hope to accomplish by winning?
- What kind of effect will this have on our relationship?
- *Why* do I want to win so badly?

Dr. Joyce Brothers once said, "There is a rule in sailing where the more maneuverable ship should give way to the less maneuverable craft. This is often a good rule to follow in human relations as well." That's a fitting analogy for leaders, isn't it? In many situations, we're the more agile ship. We all encounter difficult people on a regular basis. Sometimes they refuse to move, no matter how right we are. Their minds are closed. In situations like this, we've got to take the high road. We must be "the bigger man" and step aside. Let them pass. Otherwise a crash is inevitable.

Prideful leaders have a hard time taking the higher road. Their egos are so big that they refuse to avoid a fight they think they can win. In their minds, backing down is always a sign of weakness. We never saw this more vividly than in the leadership of Adolf Hitler. He ended up losing World War II because he wasn't able to fight a successful war on two fronts: the east and the west. By the end of his life, he was unable to negotiate anything and unable to back down for fear of admitting weakness. He ended up committing suicide because he saw no other alternative. How sad.

Most Pyrrhic Victories aren't caused by poor tactics or bad planning. They're caused by pride. Pride keeps a leader from having a realistic view of himself. It leads to overconfidence and ultimately to defeat. Pride often leads us to seek revenge and fight the wrong battles. When others hurt us, it's hard not to strike back. Many times, our first response is to get even.

In situations like this, it's helpful to remember a truth my friend John Maxwell calls the Pain Principle: hurting people naturally hurt people and are easily hurt by them. That person who keeps saying hurtful things to you may be deeply wounded inside. You don't win by pounding them into the ground. You win by showing them love and understanding that their wounds need time to heal. Look past their faults and see their needs.

Good leaders don't fight every battle. They fight the right ones. Their wisdom helps them count the costs before they engage in conflict. Their humility helps them take the high road and know their limits. As a result, they avoid Pyrrhic Victories and strengthen their relationships with others.

REFLECT AND RESPOND

In our determination to win, it's possible to lose more than we gain. A leader must count the cost before the conflict. It takes discernment and patience to know which battles are worth the fight.

1. When a disagreement arises between people, leaders must grasp the big picture, and see beyond the immediate conflict. What enables a leader to do this?

_____

_____

_____

2. Have you ever noticed that people who display wisdom are generally more patient in their demeanor? When others offend us, why is it so hard to show patience in that moment?

_____

_____

_____

3. Reflect on the rule in sailing that was used as an analogy to leadership. Which vessel best describes you? Would you typically be the "more maneuverable ship"—willing to step aside to avoid a crash? Or would you be in the category of the "less maneuverable craft"—refusing to move, regardless of the consequences because you know you are right? Give a personal example that illustrates your answer.

_____

_____

_____

4. Describe some ways to avoid a Pyrrhic Victory.

_____

_____

_____

1. Have you ever won a Pyrrhic Victory? What were the consequences?

_____

_____

_____

2. There are a lot of reasons why we argue. Many times we do it to seek a genuine resolution. But other times our arguments are fueled by ulterior motives. Here are some of the worst reasons why we fight:

   • *Fighting to fight* – you have no real purpose, you just enjoy conflict.

   • *Fighting to dominate* – you want to control others and avoid appearing weak.

   • *Fighting to save face* – you want to maintain your reputation and not look bad.

   • *Fighting to retaliate* – you want to make others look bad.

   • *Fighting to boost self-esteem* – you want to feel better about yourself, and winning helps.

   Can you relate to any of these? Which one do you struggle with the most?

_____

_____

_____

EXERCISE

Leaders can't afford to take Pyrrhic Victories lightly. When a co-worker or friend or family member has been offended, be aware that the relationship may never be recovered. Realize that it takes time and effort to re-establish a connection with that person. Why not choose to be the "bigger man" (or woman) and be willing to step aside to avoid a fatal crash?

Who are the people in your life that you argue with the most? Are your arguments productive, or are they causing more harm than good? Take some time this week to reflect on these relationships. Try to determine the true source of the conflict, and choose to have an attitude of humility when you communicate with them. Begin to make the necessary adjustments to restore and maintain a peaceful relationship.

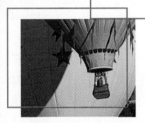

Hot Air Balloons

HOT AIR BALLOONS RISE AS THE BURNER IS RELEASED... BUT EVENTUALLY THEY
BEGIN TO FALL AND NEED TO BE REFILLED. THEY MUST CONTINUE TO BE FILLED
IN ORDER TO GO UP. PEOPLE ARE LIKE THIS. THEY MUST BE CONSISTENTLY
ENCOURAGED IN ORDER TO REACH THEIR HIGHEST POTENTIAL.

Early one Sunday morning in 1993, five passengers and a pilot boarded a hot air
balloon. Their destination was Aspen Valley, one of Colorado's popular tourist
locations. Tours like this were common, and the pilot was familiar with the area.
But on this particular morning the balloon was flown dangerously low. As the wind
began to pick up, the balloon started drifting closer and closer to a group of power
lines. Eye witnesses reported that they saw the balloon begin to rise, but it was too
little, too late. It collided with a power station and all six people on board were killed.
Although the pilot was experienced, he neglected to carry out a fundamental task:
filling the balloon enough so it could rise to a safe altitude. If only the pilot had
refilled the balloon sooner—the tragedy could have been easily avoided.

Without being refilled on a consistent basis, hot air balloons eventually fall and
crash. Hydrogen isn't just a nice option, it's a necessity. It's the same way with
people—we all need encouragement. One of the most important ways we connect
with others is by lifting them up.

We fill other people's balloons by affirming them, meeting their emotional needs,
and giving them hope. The word "encourage" literally means "to inspire courage."
It goes much deeper than just creating warm fuzzy feelings. It's about helping others
overcome obstacles, see a new perspective, and reach for their highest potential. It
has been said, "Encouragement is the oxygen of the soul."

We tend to think of encouragement like it's a luxury. It's nice to have... but we can
get by without it. However, reports from the Korean War seem to suggest otherwise.
During the 1950s, this military conflict produced the worst Prisoner of War
(POW) stories of any war in U.S. history. The death rate of American POWs was
alarmingly high, depression rates were high, and suicides were high.

Interestingly, the war camp conditions weren't especially cruel. In fact, the detainees endured relatively minor amounts of physical torture. It didn't add up, and Dr. William E. Mayer set out to discover why. His study yielded some surprising results: the men were dying because they had simply lost the will to live. The North Koreans had discovered the ultimate weapon of war: withholding all emotional support from others. No word of encouragement was ever spoken.

Soldiers only received negative letters from home, such as news of a family member's death, a notice of divorce, or overdue bill notifications. Any positive notes were withheld. Their captors rewarded them for snitching on one another and even required the men to confess their deepest faults before the entire group. Any sense of hope was completely torn away. The effects were devastating. Not only did the prisoners stop caring about one another, they stopped caring about themselves. It was not uncommon to see a prisoner go off into a corner, sit alone, and wait to die.[1]

Most of these soldiers would have likely survived if they had received some encouragement. But instead, their hope slowly withered away. Their balloons were never filled. They couldn't live off of the compliments they'd received in the past. Why? Because people never stop needing to be encouraged, the same way balloons need continuous air! Just because you praised someone in the past doesn't mean that person is set for life. Others need to know that you value them right now.

Former Ford chairman Donald Peterson understood this important principle and made a practice of jotting down positive notes to his associates every day. He once said, "Too often, people we genuinely like have no idea how we feel about them. Too often, we think: *I haven't said anything critical; why do I have to say something positive?*" We forget that without consistent encouragement, people's balloons will slowly deflate. Get this. The number one reason people leave their jobs: they don't feel appreciated; 61 percent of Americans received no praise in the workplace last year.[2]

Tom Rath and Donald Clifton developed a helpful analogy for understanding encouragement in their book, *How Full is Your Bucket: Strategies for Life and Work*. They describe it like this: "Everyone has an invisible bucket. We are at our best when our buckets are overflowing—and at our worst when they are empty. Everyone also has an invisible dipper. In each interaction, we can use our dipper either to fill or to dip from others' buckets. Whenever we fill others' buckets, we in turn fill our own."[3]

It's a simple concept, but it has some profound implications. Each time you relate to someone else, you have a choice: you can either build them up or tear them down. If you're not intentionally "filling others' buckets," you might unknowingly be dipping from them. If you're feeling discouraged, don't go around projecting that on others. Instead, build others up. You'll find that your own outlook will improve as you pour into others.

Some Advice on Giving Compliments

Encouragement rarely happens by accident. Like any skill, it takes time and effort to develop. Here are a few tips on how you can improve your compliments:

Make them Sincere

Don't you hate it when someone compliments you, but you know they don't really mean it? You wish they wouldn't have said anything in the first place, because it's just not real. Our compliments should be genuine. When they aren't, we undermine our message and actually end up doing more harm than good. I recently ran across a story that illustrates this point well:

Connie works for a major bank. Her department did a phenomenal job, making hundreds of thousands of dollars for the bank, and Connie's boss sent an e-mail congratulating and thanking her. That very afternoon, he rode the elevator with her and didn't even acknowledge her existence. It completely wiped out any good his e-mail could have done.[4]

Make Them Specific

Generic: Matt, good job on your presentation the other day.

Specific: Matt, I was so impressed with your presentation in English class yesterday! You're a very gifted public speaker, and funny too. That story you told about your family was hilarious!

Keep in mind: it doesn't take a lot of effort to get specific when we compliment others, but it can pay off huge dividends.

Make Them Public

"The Limited" retail stores have been known for going all out in their award ceremonies. One year the company invited its top 100 managers to assemble in Colorado, where they were taken via ski-lift to the top of a mountain. Each one was then publicly honored for his/her accomplishments. Video cameras captured the entire event, and the footage was used to inspire other employees. Memorable? You bet![5]

If you don't have a mountain, that's okay. There are plenty of ways that you can honor others in public:

- Affirm others when introducing them to someone else.

- When someone compliments you as a leader, deflect that praise onto your team.

- Practice reverse gossip—say positive things behind others' backs. It'll get back to them.

Make Them Personal

Complimenting someone without getting personal is kind of like sending a birthday card without ever writing anything inside. Oh sure, Hallmark may say it more eloquently, but the part we all look for is that little note scribbled in the corner. It may not be polished (or even legible!) but it's the personal touch that counts.

Try to compliment others in a way that is meaningful to them. Some people respond really well to the spoken word. Others are more receptive to e-mail messages or handwritten notes. For some, a pat on the back is far more meaningful than any sort of award ceremony could ever be. The point is that no two people are exactly alike, so tailor your compliments accordingly.

When to Encourage Others

Have you ever wondered how a hot air balloon reaches its destination? I mean, there doesn't seem to be any real way of steering the thing. The answer is quite simple actually—its heading is determined by its height. At different altitudes the wind current changes, thus affecting which direction the balloon flies. A skilled balloonist knows this and releases the burner at just the right time. If the timing's wrong, the balloon can drift dangerously off course.

Timing plays a big role in the effectiveness of our encouragement as well. Good leaders know this and have an almost intuitive sense of when to adjust altitude with their people. It's great to know *how* to encourage others, but it's also important to know *when*.

There's no one-size-fits-all guide to know the best times to encourage others, but here's a starter:

- *After they fail* – so they won't give up hope.

- *After they succeed* – so they'll want to win again.

- *When they least expect it* – so they'll know it's not an act.

- *When they first meet you* – so they won't forget your connection.

Reflect and Respond

"Encouragement is the oxygen of the soul." People are like hot air balloons when it comes to the encouragement factor. Hot air balloons need to be continuously refilled with hydrogen in order to soar high in the sky. Likewise, people need to be consistently encouraged in order to reach their highest potential.

1. As you read the stories about the Korean War POWs, how would you explain the connection between encouragement and success?

_____

_____

_____

_____

2. One of the most important ways we connect with others is by lifting them up. As a leader, who or what are you most likely to point people toward during times of crisis? Why?

_____

_____

_____

_____

3. Like any skill, it takes intentional effort to speak encouraging words to your family, friends and team members. Think of a particular person and practice giving him or her a genuine compliment. Remember to make it sincere, specific, public and personal.

_____

_____

_____

_____

Self-Assessment

1. How would you rate yourself as an encourager?
   < POOR 1 2 3 4 5 6 7 8 9 10 EXCELLENT >

2. Why did you give yourself that score?

_____

_____

_____

_____

3. What's one thing you could do to improve in this area?

_____

_____

_____

_____

_____

4. Each time you relate to others, you have a choice to build them up or tear them down. In the analogy of the invisible bucket and dipper, do you tend to pour into others or dip from others' buckets? Explain your answer with a personal example.

_____

_____

_____

_____

_____

Exercise

Years ago, an experiment was conducted to measure people's capacity to endure pain. How long could a bare-footed person stand in a bucket of ice water? It was discovered that when there was someone else present, offering encouragement and support, the person standing in the ice water could tolerate pain twice as long as when there was no one present.

Find a pad of Post-it notes, grab a pen, and take some time this week to jot down a few words of encouragement. Think about the network of people around you—your friends, teachers, team members, or work associates who most need a word of encouragement right now. Express your gratitude for having them in your life and compliment them on some positive traits you've noticed. Don't worry about writing the "perfect words"—just make your notes heartfelt and to the point.

[The Velvet Covered Brick]

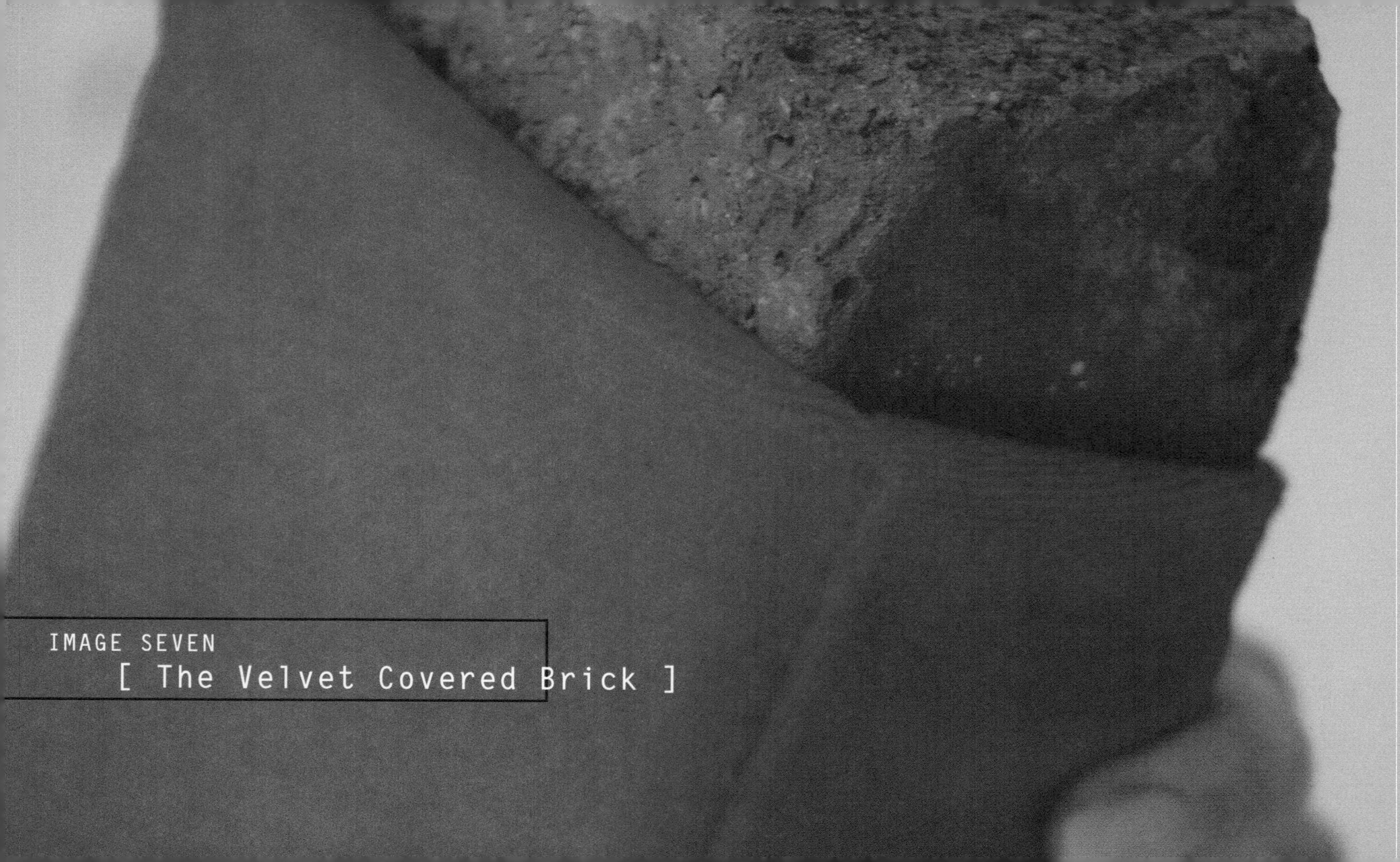

IMAGE SEVEN

[The Velvet Covered Brick]

The Velvet Covered Brick

GOOD LEADERS POSSESS BOTH STRENGTH AND SENSITIVITY. THEY ARE TOUGH AND TENDER. THEY ARE SOFT ON THE OUTSIDE (RELATIONAL), BUT FIRM AS A BRICK ON THE INSIDE (PRINCIPLE-CENTERED). BECAUSE THEY ARE EMOTIONALLY SECURE, THEY'RE ABLE TO HANDLE CONFRONTATION AND CONFLICT IN A HEALTHY WAY.

Chip Bell, author of *Magnetic Service: Secrets for Creating Passionately Devoted Customers*,[1] talks about attending a large corporate meeting where the CEO stood in front of hundreds of his managers and reported his company's financial history and projected goals. It was strong, well-scripted, and gave clear direction for the future. The scene was a carbon-copy of a zillion other big-deal annual meetings held in hundreds of ballrooms around the world. But then—something happened that took the meeting into new territory.

Without warning, the CEO moved beyond the teleprompter to the edge of the stage. The speech changed from one of pragmatism to one of passion. When he began to talk about the value of their vision and the power of every team member, he had to choke back tears. Overflowing emotion necessitated several long pauses to regain composure. He bared his soul as he spoke of specific people who had made a difference on the team. As he finished, there was a long silence. The audience sat overwhelmed by what they had just witnessed. Then they leapt to their feet for an awkwardly long standing ovation. Even the tech guys at the sound board were on their feet clapping. This was one different speech.

Bell remembers it wasn't just the CEO's tears that moved his audience. It was his courage to be unabashedly authentic, to be publicly real. Leaders too often associate their mantle of authority with a requirement for detachment. This leader broke the mold. I believe people today long for leaders who are both strong and sensitive. We're complete when our strength leads to sensitivity.

Over the years, I have served as a leader in a for-profit company, three not-for-profit organizations, and two local churches. In every context, I've observed the innate human need people have for leadership that's both tough and tender:

- *In Confrontation*—I needed to be forthright and yet encouraging.

- *In Vision-casting*—I needed to be clear and rational, yet possess "ethos" and passion.

- *In Equipping*—I needed to be practical, yet genuine and humane.

- *In Priorities*—I needed to be disciplined, yet flexible.

- *In Managing Relationships*—I needed to be principled, yet warm.

When it comes to dealing with people, the velvet covered brick approach is essential. It's easy to be one or the other—the velvet or the brick. This results in poor or weak leadership. Recently, at one company in Washington, the employees met in a conference room during a difficult season. There, the managers abruptly read aloud the names of forty people they planned to fire. They made this announcement the day before the December holiday party. Ugh. At Fob, Inc. in Chicago, employees in a staff meeting were told to go to their desks and check their e-mail. Three dozen of them were sent e-mails telling them that they had been dismissed.[2] Ouch. I heard about one retailer who was confronted by a team member about Barb, a destructive staff person who was violating company policy and values. In fact, she was causing division on the team. The manager just smiled and said, "Oh, that's just Barb. I don't have time to deal with petty issues like that." Slowly, team members began to resign because of Barb. Interesting. What makes a leader mishandle tough situations like these? They don't have the backbone to do it right.

Think for a moment about the great leaders you've observed during your lifetime. The ones we most respect are generally velvet covered bricks. They have a tough and tender side. We saw this in Mayor Rudy Giuliani after the September 11, 2001 attacks on New York City. He was tough and clear as a commander in his direction to city workers, but he was as tender as a chaplain when he attended the funeral services of citizens from the city. We saw it in Herb Kelleher, former CEO at Southwest Airlines, who was a stickler about the values of that airline, but displayed warmth and a sense of humor with his employees. President Ronald Reagan displayed some velvet covered brick qualities as he handled the Cold War and U.S. economic woes with firm convictions, yet had charisma in front of people who questioned his policies.

COMPARE AND CONTRAST

Let's further define what we mean by the "velvet covered brick" for a moment. Following are two columns that illustrate the paradoxical qualities leaders must have:

THE BRICK	THE VELVET
Tough	*Tender*
Doing right	*Being real*

Confronts destructive problems	Considers diverse perspectives
Demonstrates strength and courage	Demonstrates sensitivity and care
A stickler for results	A stickler for relationships
Is virile	Is vulnerable
Extremely professional	Extremely personal
Secure enough to take criticism	Secure enough to serve the critic
Possesses convictions about principles	Possesses compassion for people
Always embraces the responsibility	Rarely enforces the rank of the position

When do we most appreciate a velvet covered brick? During times of conflict. Leaders who can remain balanced, poised, and maintain a good perspective are the best leaders when relationships go sour. In 1983, I began working for Dr. John C. Maxwell. He modeled this principle well. As a new pastor in Lancaster, Ohio, he met a stubborn man named Jim, who was a member of his church. Jim had been responsible for running off the last two pastors at this church. His attitude stunk and his influence was consistently negative. John asked to meet with Jim, and when he did, John got acquainted with him, thanked him for meeting with him—then proceeded to engage Jim about his behavior. Basically, John said to him, "Jim, I have heard from some of our members that you haven't gotten along with the last two leaders here at this church. I also know that you've been influential at this church for many years. Now, the way I see it—you and I could fight over who gets his own way for the next several years; we could make it hell for each other here at this church. Or, we could work together. Jim—I'd like to propose we work together. By that, I mean I'd like to take you to lunch every Tuesday and talk over every major decision with you. You're smart and have influence here. I would welcome your being a part of the direction of this church. Together, I think we could see our greatest days ahead."

John paused, and went on. "Jim—you are 65 years old and it seems to me you have a choice ahead of you. Let's imagine for a moment you decide to work with me, and you have ten more years of helpful service. You could die knowing the ten best years of your life were spent helping a young pastor who desperately needed what you have to offer. Or, you could fight me at every turn, die, and know that your last ten years were spent in a bitter battle with a young man trying to lead this church. Jim, I hope you'll help me. I need you."

At that point, Jim stood up and walked out the door. John Maxwell wasn't sure where he was going or what weapon he may be retrieving... so he followed him out. Jim was hunched over the drinking fountain for what seemed like an eternity. When he stood up and turned around, John realized what was going on inside of Jim. His face was red and bathed in tears. He grabbed John and not only hugged him, he picked him up and said, "Pastor—from now on, I'm in your corner."

Following that day, Jim was a changed man. He was alert and served alongside every decision made in that church. Interestingly, he lived another ten years and died at

75 years old. His wife approached John Maxwell after the funeral, weeping. She said, "Pastor John, the last thing Jim said to me was, 'These last ten years serving in this church were the best years of my life.'"

CONFRONTATION 101

What made those years so good for Jim? A young twenty-something leader who was a velvet covered brick. He was strong enough to confront a tough situation, but sensitive enough to do it with diplomacy and out of genuine relationship. When facing conflict or when someone has done wrong, here are some basic steps I use to confront the people involved:

A. **WAIT UNTIL YOUR INITIAL ANGER SUBSIDES.**
   (Postpone any confrontation until you can be objective.)

B. **INITIATE THE CONTACT.**
   (Don't blame them and wait for them to make things right.)

C. **AFFIRM THEM AS YOU BEGIN.**
   (Thank them for meeting with you and affirm what you can.)

D. **TELL THEM YOU ARE STRUGGLING WITH A PROBLEM.**
   (Own it; it's your problem, not just theirs.)

E. **OUTLINE THE PROBLEM; ADMIT YOU DON'T UNDERSTAND.**
   (Clarify; give them the benefit of the doubt.)

F. **SHARE THE PRINCIPLE THAT IS AT STAKE.**
   (Compromise on opinions but don't violate principles.)

G. **ENCOURAGE THEM TO RESPOND.**
   (Listen well; take notes and understand their perspective.)

H. **ESTABLISH FORGIVENESS AND REPENTANCE, IF NECESSARY.**
   (Create a game plan for change.)

I. **AFFIRM YOUR LOVE AND RESPECT FOR THEM.**
   (End with words of encouragement and friendship.)

This requires emotional security. In 1860, Abraham Lincoln won the Republican nomination over three more highly qualified candidates. Each had more experience, and were household names in the U.S. These rivals were shocked to lose to this backwoods lawyer. Lincoln, however, stunned everyone when he turned around and invited all three to serve on his cabinet. It was a dangerous move, but he later said, "We needed the strongest men in the Cabinet. We needed to hold our own people together. I had looked the party over and concluded that these were the very strongest men. Then I had no right to deprive the country of their service."[3] Now that's a velvet covered brick.

Great leaders have both a tough and tender side; they are strong yet sensitive. I call it the velvet covered brick approach to leadership. Today's leaders need to be relational with people—soft like velvet on the outside. But they also need to hold fast to their principles—firm like a brick on the inside.

1. Think about some great leaders you've observed who have adopted the velvet covered brick style of leadership. Describe a time when they balanced the paradox of being both tough and tender.

_____

_____

_____

_____

_____

_____

2. In contrast, what pitfalls have you observed about leaders who fail to embrace the velvet covered brick style of leadership?

_____

_____

_____

_____

_____

3. From the "Confrontation 101" section of this Habitude, list three steps that are the most difficult for you to put into practice.

_____

_____

_____

_____

_____

_____

Self-Assessment

Often, leaders are either too tough or too tender. Which are you? Corporate psychologists have labeled leadership responses to conflict with animal names. Find the one you most identify with:

- ○ **Sharks** (I really like to get my own way; I win and you may lose, but it's better this way.)

- ○ **Foxes** (We have to compromise; everyone wins a little and loses a little.)

- ○ **Turtles** (I don't like conflict and I tend to withdraw and not face it.)

- ○ **Teddy Bears** (I'll make peace however I can; I don't mind losing so you can win.)

- ○ **Owls** (Let's work at this and find a way in which everyone can win.)

Give some examples of why you chose the animal you did.

_____

_____

_____

_____

_____

_____

_____

Exercise

Consider the tough decisions and tough people you face right now. How have you handled them up to this point? What two steps could you take to demonstrate both the tough and the tender side of leadership? How can you get to the right result, but sustain the right relationship with the people who are part of the conflict? Determine what those steps are and take them this week. Report back to your group how things went.

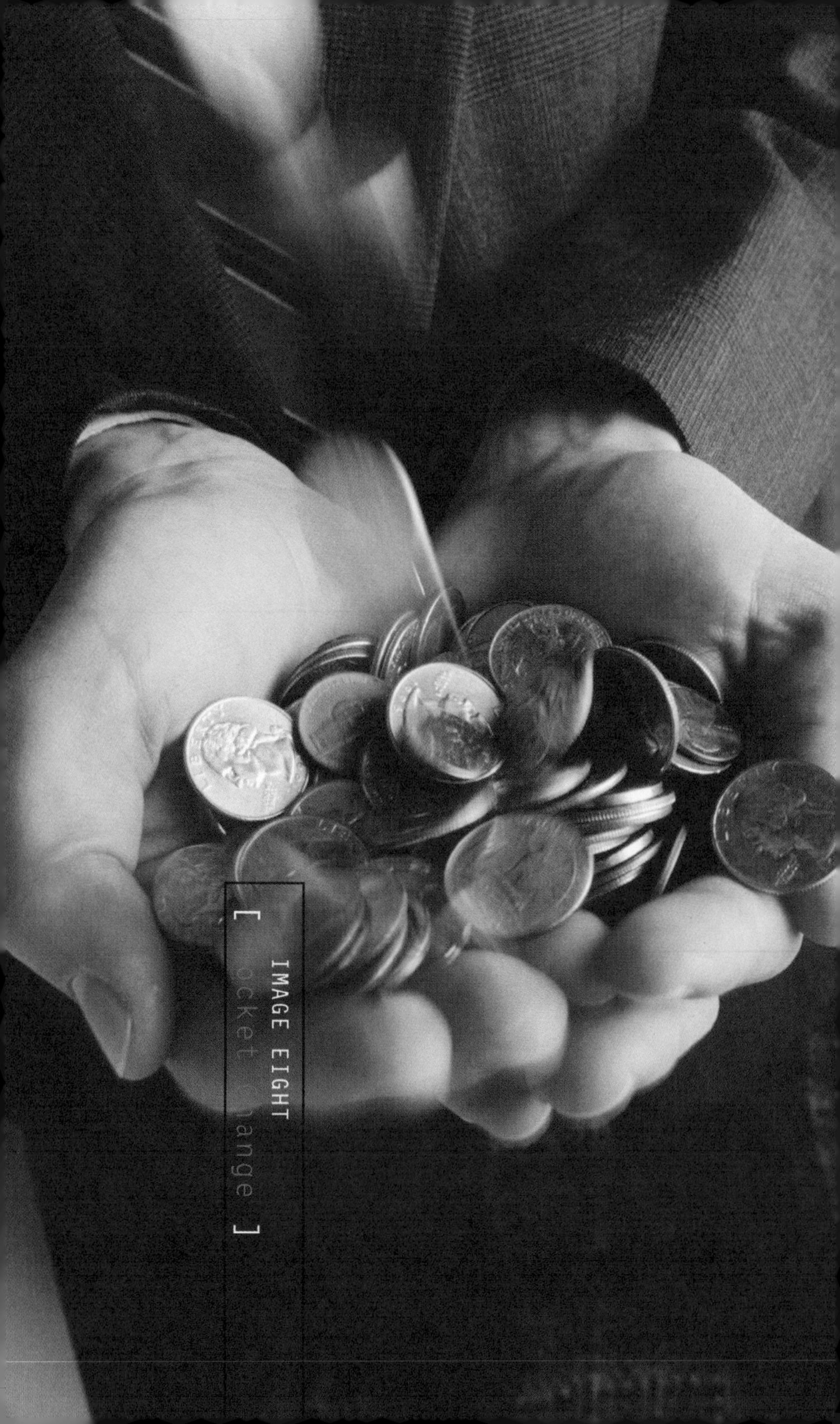
IMAGE EIGHT

Pocket Change

LEADERS EARN CREDIBILITY WITH OTHERS BY DISPLAYING INTEGRITY AND MAKING WISE
DECISIONS. THIS PUTS EMOTIONAL CHANGE IN THEIR POCKET AND ENHANCES THEIR
INFLUENCE. IF LEADERS FAIL TO DO THIS, THEY LOSE THE CHANGE IN THEIR POCKET
WITH PEOPLE. LEADERS ARE CONSTANTLY FILLING OR EMPTYING THEIR POCKETS.

This Habitude explains one of the greatest mysteries of leadership. I have watched
countless leaders enter a new position and go through a "honeymoon" period.
Everything is new, people are optimistic, expectations are high. Then, over time,
things change. Momentum wanes. People aren't as excited as they once were. Often,
the leader doesn't understand the loss of momentum, so he explains it away by saying,
"Well, I can't expect things to stay fresh forever. Honeymoons don't last a lifetime."

Sometimes, however, the diminishing excitement has little to do with a honeymoon
ending. These leaders miss what is really happening. They fail to recognize this
Habitude at work. I call it "change in your pocket," and I first learned it from my
long-time mentor, John Maxwell. Every leader begins a job with some change in
his or her pocket. You might call it emotional change. It's "social capital" the leader
can use in relationships to get things done, to influence others, to make programs
happen. Each time that leader makes a decision which involves others, some of that
change in his or her pocket is spent. If the decision goes well, those people return
the change. If things go really well, the leader gets extra change back!

In other words, leaders maintain or gain credibility with others when they choose
wisely and demonstrate integrity. When a leader continually leads with wisdom and
integrity, tons of change accumulates in his or her pocket, enough to endure a rainy
day or two when things don't go so well. As a leader, the name of the game in
relationships is to possess lots of change.

My wife and I lived in an apartment complex the first four years of our marriage. For
a while, we did our laundry at a laundromat that required quarters to wash and dry
our clothes. I remember the frustration of showing up with several loads of clothes—
and being just shy of the number of quarters I needed to get my clothes clean and
dry. On a cold December night, it was extra frustrating to not have enough change!

Today, I live just north of Atlanta, Georgia. I drive a state freeway every week called Georgia 400. It's a toll road. It costs 50 cents to pass through. There's nothing more embarrassing than arriving at the toll booth and realizing you've got no change in your pocket! What do you do? Do you scrounge through the car looking for dimes and nickels while the other cars wait? Do you try to back up and find an ATM? Do you break through the crossbar and hope no one sees you? Trust me. I know. This situation is embarrassing.

In the same way, some leaders enter a decision period unprepared. For instance, they may lead a committee meeting and want to propose a new idea. They believe everyone will just love this idea. But, alas, no one votes for it. They are stunned. They wonder what happened. Did that group of people all of the sudden turn on them? No, it wasn't all of the sudden. Over time, that leader likely was losing change in his pocket, and by that meeting, he had no credibility to lead anyone. Usually, leaders lose their pocket change slowly over time and don't realize it. In fact, former Secretary of State Colin Powell suggests that leaders must look for symptoms of this happening among their people.

What are the signs of a loss of trust? Powell remembers as a military officer, "The day soldiers stop bringing you their problems is the day you have stopped leading them. They have either lost confidence that you can help them or concluded that you do not care. Either case is a failure of leadership."[1]

Most leaders lose the change in their pocket by lacking integrity. Their own dishonesty becomes a hole in their pocket, and others lose respect for them. Out of history comes the story of a frontier preacher whose two sons talked him into taking in a stray dog. The dog was black as coal except for three distinctive white hairs on his tail. One day, they saw an ad in the local newspaper for a lost dog which fit the dog's description perfectly, including the white hairs. With the help of his boys, that preacher carefully pulled out the three white hairs. Later, the owner heard this preacher had a dog who fit his dog's description and traveled over looking for him. When the owner arrived, the dog showed every sign of recognizing him. Naturally, the owner wanted to take him home.

The preacher asked, "Didn't you say your dog had three white hairs on his tail?" The owner, unable to find the hairs, was forced to leave. Those young boys watched their dad's deception at work. Later, the preacher wrote, "I kept the dog, but I lost my boys." The names of his two boys were Frank and Jesse James—infamous criminals as adults. During their childhood, their dad was unable to positively influence them, regardless of how good his sermons were. Why? There was a hole in his pocket, and he lost all of his change. He didn't notice because his sons still hung out with him. Sadly, they no longer respected him. Keep in mind: there's a difference between being liked as a friend and being followed as a leader. If people don't respect you—you won't lead them.

So what does a leader look like who continues to accumulate change in his pocket? One example is John Wooden, legendary basketball coach for UCLA during my boyhood years. He was both capable and reliable; he did well and he did right for years and years. He won ten NCAA championships while at UCLA. No one else has come close to that achievement. "Discipline yourself and others won't need to," Wooden would say to his team. "Never lie, cheat, or steal… and earn the right to be proud and confident."

One of his rules was no facial hair. "Beards take too long to dry and you could catch a cold leaving the gym," he'd say. This rule drove some players crazy. One day, All-American center Bill Walton showed up with a full beard. "It's my right," he insisted. Wooden told Walton that he admired someone who stood up for what he believed. Then he smiled and said, "We're going to miss you, Bill." Walton shaved it right then and there. Now, Walton calls once a week to tell Coach Wooden he loves him. And he's not alone. Of the 180 players who played for Wooden, he knows the whereabouts of 172 of them. Of course, it's not hard since most of them call on a regular basis.[2]

Now what enables this kind of relationship and respect? John Wooden has tons of change in his pocket with everyone who knows him. In fact, I'd say John Wooden has the equivalent of Fort Knox in his pockets. His wisdom and integrity have kept his pockets free from any holes. Now, he has credibility with anyone he meets.

REFLECT AND RESPOND

Leaders gain credibility with others when they display integrity and make wise decisions. This credibility is like putting emotional change into the leader's pocket. When pocket change accumulates, a leader's influence escalates. But the reverse is also true. Dishonesty or poor decisions result in less pocket change and diminished influence.

1. Reflecting on a leader that you admire, give an example of how he/she has gained pocket change, earning credibility in the eyes of their team.

_____

_____

_____

2. Write down some of the ways that leaders throughout history have lost pocket change. How did they get a hole in their pocket, losing credibility?

_____

_____

_____

3. Do you agree that leaders gain respect more by their actions than by their words? Why or why not? Share an example from your own life.

_____

_____

_____

Evaluate the change you have in your own pocket with others by answering these questions:

1. When a problem has to be solved, do others look to you? Which is more true about you: Are you simply looked at as a friend, or do people respect and follow you as a leader?

_____

_____

_____

2. What are the signs of others losing trust in you and your leadership?

_____

_____

_____

3. What's your track record for decision-making? Do you have a history of wise or unwise decisions? Do you follow through on your decisions?

_____

_____

_____

EXERCISE

This week, try these practices to earn the respect of others and to increase your pocket change:

1. CONSISTENCY: Be consistent in returning phone calls, in your moods, and in your communication. *Integrity means keeping your commitment even when your circumstances have changed.*

2. QUALITY DECISION-MAKING: Reflect; seek counsel to make wise choices, communicate them well. *Demonstrate you have others' best interests in mind when you make tough decisions.*

3. GETTING ALONG WITH PEOPLE: Show them you trust them; give them the benefit of the doubt, and they'll do the same for you. Learn to relate to all kinds of people and connect with them. *These steps will not only exhibit respect for others, but it will gain their respect for you in return.*

The Waldorf Principle

THE WAY TO THE TOP WITH PEOPLE IS BY SERVING THEM EXTRAVAGANTLY AND
SACRIFICIALLY. A SIMPLE CLERK DID THIS TO MR. WALDORF, AND THE RICH
TYCOON RETURNED TO MAKE THAT CLERK HIS FIRST HOTEL MANAGER IN NEW
YORK. PEOPLE EXPECT GOOD SERVICE FROM LEADERS. THEY ARE SURPRISED
WHEN WE SERVE SACRIFICIALLY.

One stormy night many years ago, an elderly man and his wife entered the lobby
of a small hotel in Philadelphia. Trying to get out of the rain, the couple approached
the front desk, hoping to get some shelter for the night.

"We'd like a room, please," the husband requested. The clerk, a friendly man with
a winning smile, looked at the couple and explained that there were three
conventions in town. "All of our rooms are taken," the clerk said. "But I can't send
a nice couple like you out in the rain at one o'clock in the morning. Would you
perhaps be willing to sleep in my room? It's not exactly a suite, but it will be good
enough to make you folks comfortable for the night."

When the couple declined, the clerk insisted. "Don't worry about me; I'll make out
just fine," he told them. So the couple agreed to spend the night in his room. As
he paid his bill the next morning, the elderly man said to the clerk, "You're an
exceptional man. Finding people who are both friendly and helpful is rare these
days. You are the kind of manager who should be the boss of the best hotel in the
United States. Maybe someday I'll build one for you."

Two years passed. The clerk was still working at the hotel in Philadelphia when he
received a letter from the old man. It recalled that stormy night, and enclosed was
a round-trip ticket to New York, asking the young man to pay him a visit.

The old man met him in New York and led him to the corner of Fifth Avenue and
34th Street. He then pointed to a great new building there, a palace of reddish stone,
with turrets and watchtowers thrusting up to the sky. "That," he said, "is the hotel
I'd like you to manage."

The old man's name was William Waldorf Astor, and the magnificent structure was the original Waldorf-Astoria Hotel. The clerk who became its first manager was George C. Boldt. This young clerk never foresaw how his simple act of sacrificial service would lead him to become the manager of one of the world's most glamorous hotels.

The way to the top with people is not just through service. It's through extravagant, sacrificial service. When someone goes out of their way to help you, it makes all the difference in the world.

- It's the difference between a grumpy, inattentive waitress versus a professional, friendly server whom you actually enjoy talking to and who allows a special order.

- It's the difference between calling customer support and plowing through automated menus versus being instantly connected to a live person who goes out of her way to help.

- It's the difference between a professor who just tolerates your questions versus having one who spends extra time and effort to help you really grasp the material.

When others do their very best to serve us, their influence increases. We don't look down on them for serving us. On the contrary, our respect level for them rises. We're often so impressed that we start considering ways we can serve them in return! Their attitude and initiative is attractive. As I discuss this with people, few disagree with the idea. However, many don't buy it. Most don't serve others this way because they fear being looked down upon. They struggle with pride. They feel that serving others creates a view of them that is lower; after all—those at the top are being served! Let me play a little game with you to show how wrong this assumption is.

Question: In your past, who has served you more than anyone else in the world? The answer for most of us is our mother. Moms usually do anything to serve their kids. Now, think about this. Do you think **less** of your mother for serving you, or **more** of her? My guess is that your love and respect for her goes up when she sacrificially serves.

It's no different with us. When we serve others, our influence increases as well. My friend Zig Ziglar is famous for saying, "You can have everything in life you want if you will just help enough other people get what they want!" It's true. He's one of the most humble servant-leaders I've ever met, and he's at the top of his field.

He's not the only one. Most of the great leaders I've run across have embraced the Waldorf Principle. Case in point: When Michael Eisner was CEO of Disney, his job description included "trash collecting." Just imagine, the CEO of a multi-billion-dollar organization, picking up trash at his own theme park. Think about the kind of effect that must have had on his employees. He could have just ordered someone else to do it.

It's ironic. You'd think that true influence would come through force—ordering others around and letting people know you're the boss. But just the opposite is true. Real influence comes through humbly serving others. It's one of the greatest leadership paradoxes in existence.

Paths to Power

There are all sorts of ways you can go about achieving influence. Some of them are better than others. Take a look at the following list and see if you can identify the model you use most. I've ordered them from worst to best.

7. Force

People follow you because they feel threatened and are overpowered. They move unwillingly and are quick to rebel if given the chance. Unhealthy governments rule by force. It's the worst path to power.

6. Manipulation

People follow you because you coerce them. You use words to trick them and back them into a corner. They have no choice. Folks resent being used and quickly seek a healthier environment.

5. Intimidation

People follow you because they're afraid not to. They feel emotionally bullied by you and obey because they want to avoid being fired, hurt, embarrassed, etc... This is the third worst path and is often used when quick action is needed.

4. Exchange

This is the most common path to power we use. People follow you because you can do something for them. Both parties receive something: you work, and your boss pays you. This path works, but it's still temporal. It's over when one party finds a better deal.

3. Persuasion

People follow you because they are moved to cooperation. They agree because of the ideas or incentives which you provide. This path now utilizes verbal expression which makes others want to follow you. Literally translated from its root words, "persuasion" means "through sweetness."

2. Motivation

People follow you because you create excitement. Your cause and your passion move others to action. People willingly go where they would not have gone themselves. This is an even better approach, but still not the best.

1. Honor

People follow you because you honor them through service. You and your followers have a mutual respect for each other. Others submit because you've earned their esteem. This is the best path and the longest lasting form of leadership. It earns fierce loyalty and commitment as a result.

Think again about the night that George Boldt served Mr. Waldorf and his wife. He didn't know who they were. He didn't see what they could give him in return one day. He just honored anyone who came through the door. And—he won them over. When you take the path of honor, your influence increases. Even if you don't have a formal leadership position at your school or work, you can still influence others. Martin Luther King, Jr. once said, "Everybody can be great... because anybody can serve. You don't have to have a college degree to serve. You don't have to make your subject and verb agree to serve. You only need a heart full of grace. A soul generated by love."

The Waldorf Principle reminds leaders that the way to greatness is through sacrificial and extravagant service. In November 2005, Oprah Winfrey honored some people who practiced this principle following Hurricane Katrina. After that natural disaster, thousands of victims were displaced, without a home or food. Many Americans left their own comfort to serve them—often at great expense. Maryanne Burnham was a nurse who wanted to serve the victims in Louisiana. Her hospital wouldn't give her time off to do it, so she quit her job. Serving the less fortunate was more important to her. Ryan Devin left Chicago to serve folks after the hurricane. How did he pay for his trip? He sold his World Series tickets—the tickets to watch his own Chicago White Sox play in a World Series they hadn't been to in more than 80 years! He had never missed a game in 30 years. Extravagant? Sacrificial? You bet. But if you want to connect with others, be a servant to them. Forcing influence always backfires. Earning influence through honor always pays off. Remember the simple clerk, Mr. Boldt, and take the path of a servant leader.

REFLECT AND RESPOND

Most leaders I know want their lives to count. They don't wake up in the morning and think to themselves, "Hmmm... I think I'll be mediocre today." Unfortunately, we often lose sight of what greatness truly means. True influence doesn't come through force or intimidation. Just the opposite is true. When leaders humbly serve others, their influence increases.

1. Why do you think that some leaders resist the idea of sacrificial service? If you identify with resisting servant leadership, what is your honest level of desire to change?
   a. Low   b. Medium   c. High

_____

_____

_____

_____

_____

2. Do you know anyone who models servant leadership? Are they more influential because of it? Explain.

_____

_____

_____

_____

_____

SELF-ASSESSMENT

1. What does it mean to serve sacrificially? How are you doing in this area?

_____

_____

_____

_____

_____

2. When you serve others, do you just do the bare minimum, or do you exceed their expectations?

_____

_____

_____

_____

3. Look at the "Paths to Power" list again. Which path(s) do you tend to follow most?

_____

_____

_____

_____

EXERCISE

True service always costs us something. This week, perform one act of service for someone else. But instead of just doing the bare minimum, go the extra mile. Really sacrifice yourself on someone else's behalf. Don't just clean your friend's room... clean her bathroom as well. Don't just wish him a happy birthday... organize a surprise party! Don't just write a nice note... write several notes and post them in unexpected places. Sure, it will require your time, energy, and even money, but that goes with the territory. After you're done, reflect on the experience. What did you discover?

[The Gardener's Job]

The Gardener's Job

A GARDENER'S PRIMARY JOB IS TO NURTURE THE DEVELOPMENT OF HIS PLANTS. LIKEWISE, GOOD LEADERS CENTER THEIR AGENDAS ON GROWING TEAM MEMBERS. LEADERS ARE TO BE GOOD MENTORS AND INVEST THEIR LIVES IN OTHERS. THEIR KEY JOB IS NOT DOING PROGRAMS OR DISTRIBUTING PRODUCTS, BUT DEVELOPING PEOPLE.

When it comes to domestic chores like planting, gardening, lawns and trees, one thing is for sure—I do not have a "green thumb." I do, however, recognize people who do. I have a friend who absolutely loves gardening. It's more than a hobby; it's his life. He can name every kind of flower, he knows the best time of year to plant that flower, and can tell you exactly what it needs to grow and flourish.

He has taught me a few things about gardens that bear repeating. One day while he was preparing the soil in his garden for some new begonias, he taught me how all plants have "biotic potential." This means all plants have the inherent capacity to grow, survive, and reproduce. It's in every plant. He smiled and went on, "You see—I can't grow a thing. A gardener can only create an environment that is conducive for growth, like providing rich soil, fresh water, good fertilizer, and placing the plants in a sunny or shady area, depending on where they will flourish. At that point, it's up to the good Lord." Then he smiled. "Of course, the good Lord does use us gardeners. Many plants wouldn't make it without a gardener creating the right environment."

Wise gardeners know that they must create an environment for growth. They also know this must be their primary focus: creating environments to grow plants. Similarly, good leaders approach their roles with the same priority. They are like gardeners. They can't control the growth of people or organizations, but they can construct environments that foster growth. One hundred and fifty years ago, a biologist named Justus Von Liebig discovered that four nutrients are necessary for the growth of a plant: nitrogen, lime, phosphoric acid, and potash. As long as all four minerals are present in sufficient amounts in the soil, growth happens automatically. Development stops when one or more are missing.

Human Gardeners

I believe good leaders understand the necessary ingredients to grow people. They see themselves as mentors and believe their primary task is not growing big organizations, but growing big people. Big organizations are a by-product. They focus on building people by creating environments in which others reach their potential. They are human gardeners. I experienced my first human gardener at seventeen years old. A man named Shawn Mitchell saw some potential in me as a high school student and took me under his wing. He taught me how to plan, how to build relationships and eventually how to lead. Under his leadership, a group of us rented out a music hall and showed a great movie every Friday night. Afterward, Shawn would speak on a principle we'd seen in the movie. My job each Friday night was to meet Shawn beforehand, get a preview of the evening, make sure the movie was ready, and hold his coat. I was the protégé. He was the mentor and leader.

One Friday night, Shawn met me backstage and surprised me. He whispered with a raspy voice, "Tim, I don't think I'm going to be able to speak tonight. I need you to speak tonight." I was paralyzed. I was only a junior in high school and this was a large audience. I wasn't ready to speak—my job was to observe him and hold his coat! But, alas, I had no choice. Shawn wasn't up to it, and I was the only alternative. So he gave me his notes, and that night I walked onto the stage, shaking in my shoes. Thankfully, I survived the ordeal. I actually had fun. Afterward, Shawn came to me with a big smile on his face and said, "Tim, you were great. From now on, we will take turns speaking. I will be on one Friday night, and you'll be on the next."

And that's how I got my start speaking and leading.

Interestingly, Shawn and I met just a few years ago for dinner, to reminisce about those early days in my leadership experience. We talked about my first time up in front of that audience. During our conversation, Shawn said, "Tim, I have a confession to make. I really didn't have laryngitis that night. But I couldn't think of any other way to get you up front to speak. You would have always depended on me, and I knew you could do it."

We both laughed. (Of course, I wanted to hit Shawn that night for putting me through such an ordeal.) Later, however, I became grateful for a leader who placed more importance on training a young guy like me than on having a perfect performance that particular Friday night. He was a mentor first. He was a human gardener.

Everyone Who Makes It Has a Mentor

The *Harvard Business Review* published a special edition years ago entitled, "Everyone Who Makes it has a Mentor."[1] The cover article included interviews with the top CEOs of Fortune 500 companies. They were looking for common threads in these top leaders; they found only one. The one common characteristic in these CEOs was that each had a mentor. Every single one had found a sharp "coach" whom they could call at two a.m., if necessary, to ask a question or find guidance or support. Interesting. Do you want a great team around you? Decide to be a mentor for them. Celebrities like Oprah Winfrey, Tom Brokaw, John McCain, and Cal Ripkin all point to a mentor who helped them push through mediocrity to achieve greatness. Consider this: half of the Nobel Peace Prize winners in 2004 were mentored by former Peace Prize laureates. Coincidence? I don't think so.

Mentoring is not merely for the old and wise. Every good leader assumes this role. Mentoring is simply one person empowering another by sharing their resources. Human gardeners value relationships as much as they do results. They invest time and energy in people. John Crosby once said, "A mentor is a brain to pick, a shoulder to cry on, and a kick in the seat of the pants."

So, What Does a Mentor Do?

Let me suggest six gifts that human gardeners offer their people…

1. They Paint Pictures

Most people think in pictures. If I say the word, "banana," most don't think of the letters b-a-n-a-n-a, they imagine a yellow piece of fruit. Mentors capitalize on our visual minds and paint pictures of the way leadership works by telling stories, using metaphors, or employing images (like *Habitudes!*).

2. They Provide Handles

Every door or drawer has a handle. A handle is something we can grab on to. Good mentors summarize great principles into simple terms that their mentees can get a hold of and understand. They define the principles and give practical ways they can be applied in real life.

3. They Supply Roadmaps

Road maps accomplish four goals: First, they give us the big picture. (We can see an entire state on one piece of paper). Second, they show us where we are. Third, they show us the roads we can take to reach our desired destination. Fourth, they reveal what roads to avoid. Good mentors do this, too.

4. They Furnish Laboratories

A laboratory is simply a safe place in which to experiment. Science class always includes a lab. So do good mentors. They furnish safe places for others to experiment and actually practice the principles their mentees are learning. They understand we live in an experiential generation.

5. They Give Roots

Plants can only grow as tall as their root systems grow deep. Roots represent the foundation for solid growth. They provide strength and stability;

something to stand on. These roots might take the form of a "moral compass," enabling a mentee to make wise decisions based on healthy values.

6. They Offer Wings

Finally, mentors offer wings—the ability to soar to new heights beyond where they have gone before. Wings enable mentees to think big, to attempt huge goals, to not fear taking risks. Mentors applaud as their mentees pass them up and exceed what they have done themselves.

Reflect and Respond

A simple definition of mentoring is one person empowering another by sharing their resources. The one common thread among top leaders was that each of them had a mentor, a coach that supported them and guided them through mediocrity to greatness.

1. The following acrostic describes four key ingredients in mentoring. It reminds me of the right IDEA on how to grow people:

   I – Instruction: Verbally teach how to serve and lead.

   D – Demonstration: Model how to serve and lead—do "show and tell" time with your mentee

   E – Experience: Provide "a laboratory," a first-hand experience in which to learn.

   A – Assessment: Evaluate the progress; assess what your mentee did right and wrong.

2. Identify someone you could mentor. Choose one leadership principle from the first nine Habitudes in this book that you want to share with them. Write out how you would implement the four aspects in the IDEA acrostic to help your mentee assimilate the leadership principle.

_____

_____

_____

_____

_____

_____

_____

_____

Evaluate yourself on how well you "cultivate the garden" and mentor the people around you:

1. Who are you purposefully investing in right now?

_____

_____

_____

_____

_____

2. How are you "watering" them and creating environments for growth? Assess the following:

  a. How do you paint pictures?

_____

_____

_____

  b. How do you provide handles?

_____

_____

_____

  c. How do you supply roadmaps?

_____

_____

_____

  d. How do you furnish laboratories?

_____

_____

_____

e. How do you give roots?

_____

_____

_____

f. How do you offer wings?

_____

_____

_____

EXERCISE

I believe that every leader should simultaneously have three types of people in his or her life at all times:

1. A MENTOR WHO IS INVESTING IN YOUR LIFE

2. AN ACCOUNTABILITY PARTNER WHO IS SUPPORTING YOU

3. A MENTEE, OR SOMEONE YOU ARE POURING YOUR LIFE INTO

If you haven't done this already, choose people who can fill these roles in your life—one mentor, one accountability partner, and one mentee. Then, set times to meet with them for the purpose of growth. Choose to discuss a book, practice a principle and encourage each other during this year. (Maybe you could even go through a Habitudes book with someone!) Be a gardener with people—cultivate the relationship so those people can grow.

IMAGE ELEVEN

[walker]

Tightrope Walker

IT'S EASY TO WATCH A TIGHTROPE WALKER; IT'S ANOTHER THING TO TRUST HIM
ENOUGH TO CLIMB ON HIS BACK. OUR WORLD IS FULL OF PEOPLE WHO DON'T
TRUST OTHERS. GOOD LEADERS BUILD TRUST THROUGH COMPETENCE. THEY
RECOGNIZE THE DIFFERENCE BETWEEN BEING LIKED AS A FRIEND AND BEING
FOLLOWED AS A LEADER.

Charles Blondin, the French aerialist, was one of the finest tightrope walkers of all
time. No doubt he's the most famous. In fact, he was sort of the Michael Jordan
of his day. He is best known as the one who walked a wire across Niagara Falls. On
one crossing, August 18, 1859, crowds of people watched in breathless terror as he
maneuvered across the wire and back again. Finally, he returned to the American
side to throngs of cheering fans.

The media caught it all. "You're the greatest, Blondin!" they all cried. When the
cheering subsided, Blondin thanked the people, then offered a challenge. "You think
I'm wonderful?" he teased.

"Yes!" they responded. "No one can do what you do. You can do anything!"

"Good," he replied. "Then I should have no trouble getting a volunteer for my next
act." He paused. Everyone listened. "I need someone to ride atop my shoulders as
I cross back over the falls again."

The crowd fell silent. He beckoned again that he just needed one person. Just one.
But no one volunteered. Finally, after a long pause, Blondin turned to his friend,
Harry Colcord, and said, "Harry, you will have to come with me." Harry's face turned
white. (He suffered from a fear of heights.) Hesitantly, he stepped forward and
climbed onto Blondin's shoulders. Charles and Harry then crossed over the wire
above Niagara Falls for the next 45 minutes. Six times Harry had to dismount on
the tightrope for Blondin to gather his strength—but they eventually made it.[1]

There is a great lesson to be learned from this event in history. In fact, I believe it
is a leadership lesson in one sense. It is easy to watch a tightrope walker—it's another
thing to climb on his back. Similarly, it's easy to like someone as a friend and say

you believe in him. It's quite another thing to trust him enough to follow him. Talk is cheap. The litmus test for a leader is this: Do people trust you enough to go with you on the journey? Do they follow your lead? Leadership is about building trust. All true leadership operates on the basis of trust. People only follow you as closely as they trust you.

BUILDING TRUST

So how does a leader build trust? In a word, it's through competence. Blondin demonstrated his ability to walk a tightrope before he asked anyone to climb on his back. If people believe you have strong competence (you can do what you say) and strong character (you will do what you say) then they just might follow you. But usually not until then.

A survey was taken among 13,000 employees across the country. The researchers found that only 39 percent of workers trust their senior executives in the corporate world.[2] And that number is dropping. The sad reality is that many employees believe their leaders lack both character and competence. I am glad to say I have seen great leadership during my career—and in many surprising places. While I lived in San Diego, I built a friendship with Dave, a sharp young leader who worked in the men's furnishings department of Nordstrom. Nordstrom's reputation for excellent customer service is legendary. I've experienced it over and over. I remember meeting Dave as I shopped for a new suit. I gave Dave all the specifications for the suit I was looking for. He ended up showing me three suits that fit my description. Dave then got very detailed about the features of each suit. I could tell he knew his stuff. After trying them all on, I fell in love with one of them. Dave, however, talked me out of it. (Yes, you read that correctly.) After seeing it on me, he realized it wouldn't hold its shape after several dry cleanings—so he couldn't sell it to me. He knew he'd get some more suits in the next week and offered to call me when they came in. Wow! Now that's a leader I will trust! He was competent and he performed with integrity.

I live in the South. Since moving here, I have heard countless stories of Civil War General Robert E. Lee. He practiced this Habitude. Lee led his outnumbered soldiers to many victories. He earned the label "The Silver Fox" because he outmaneuvered or outwitted his opponents so many times. Because of his success, his men were devoted to him. In fact, his men fought heroically because they loved their leader. As one of his generals, Henry Wise, told him, "Ah, General Lee, these men are not fighting for the Confederacy; they are fighting for you." He was a tightrope walker—and his army had climbed onto his back.

It is ironic that Lee's counterpart, Ulysses S. Grant, is a study in contrast. After the Union Army won the Civil War, Grant was approached to become the next U.S. president. He should have never said yes. He and a majority of others assumed his popularity would make him a good president. Wrong. Popularity is never a good substitute for leadership. He offered no vision to the country, lacked initiative, provided few ideas, and ended up with two scandalous terms in office.[3] Once again, there's a difference between being liked as a friend and being followed as a leader.

Let me take this a step further. This Habitude becomes clearer when you understand this principle:

LEADERSHIP RISES BASED UPON PROVIDING THE SCARCEST RESOURCE.

If you are part of a group of people and you possess what is most scarce and most desired—you will be the leader. Folks will look to you to lead the way. Effective leaders continue growing, and they purpose to offer something valuable to the teams on which they serve.

Case in point. During the Great Depression in 1932, Charles Darrow and his wife were among the many Americans who lost their jobs and their hope. They had nothing. Earlier, he had dreamed of becoming a millionaire, but now that seemed impossible. To keep their dream alive, Charles and his wife began playing a little game they made up each night where they pretended to have a million dollars. They would buy and sell homes and other buildings in their imagination. Realizing that this game was helping their friends keep hope alive—they developed the game for groups, creating play money, a game board, houses and hotels, game cards, and dice. In short, Charles Darrow created the game that many of us have played at some point in our lives, Monopoly. Because hope was so scarce, Charles Darrow had developed an idea to provide people with a way to keep their dreams alive... even if it was only a game. In 1935, he sold that game to Parker Brothers—and can you guess how much they paid him for it? One million dollars. He reached his own dream. Not bad for providing the scarcest resource at the time. Charles Darrow, Robert E. Lee, my friend Dave, and Charles Blondin all had people who were willing to climb on their backs. Anyone willing to trust you that way?

REFLECT AND RESPOND

It's one thing to praise a tightrope walker and cheer him on to the other side. It's another thing to trust him enough to climb on his shoulders as he maneuvers across the thin wire. The same could be said about the leadership journey. There is definitely a difference in being liked as a friend and being followed as a leader.

1. What do leaders offer that causes people to want to follow them? Do people trust you enough to follow you as their leader?

_____

_____

_____

_____

2. Consider the idea that "leadership rises based upon providing the scarcest resource." Rewrite this concept in your own words. Next, identify what resource you have that is scarce.

_____

_____

_____

_____

3. Can you name some other historical leaders or current leaders who have earned the right to be followed?

_____

_____

_____

_____

SELF-ASSESSMENT

Evaluate yourself with the list below, "Crossing the Seven Cs to Leadership." Give yourself a score of one to ten.

___ **COMPETENCE:** I know my unique abilities and use them to solve problems.

CHARACTER: I do what I should even when I don't feel like it.

COURAGE: I'm challenged to start new things and step out to initiate the process.

___ **CHARISMA:** I attract people by giving them confidence and encouragement.

___ **COMPASSION:** I'm moved to help those in need even when it costs me something.

CONVICTIONS: Others can see my strong values by the way I live my life.

COMMITMENT: I don't get distracted by obstacles, and I finish what I start.

EXERCISE

This week, concentrate on your unique abilities as they relate to your team or group. What do you offer that can meet a need—what resource do you have that is scarce? Once you've identified this resource, determine to look for ways to add value to others. Identify problems you can help solve. Use your abilities to earn the right to be followed. Now, evaluate where others put their trust. In what areas do others most quickly follow your lead? Where does your influence lie? Write out the results.

IMAGE TWELVE

[Lightning Rods]

IMAGE TWELVE
[Lightning Rods]

Lightning Rods

A LIGHTNING ROD PROTECTS A BUILDING BY SAFELY TAKING THE STRIKE AND
GROUNDING IT. IT CHANNELS THE IMPACT OF THAT STRIKE TO A SAFE PLACE.
LEADERS HANDLE ANGER AND CRITICISM IN A SIMILAR WAY. THEY TAKE THE HEAT
FOR THE TEAM, AND THEY FIND APPROPRIATE OUTLETS FOR THEIR OWN ANGER.

Two years ago, my hometown in Atlanta endured an extremely harsh thunderstorm.
It was like we were in the movies. Lightning flashed and thunder crashed, trees fell
down, some rooftops were ruptured, and power lines were out for days. It took over
a week to get the city cleaned up and running again. Everyone saw the power of
Mother Nature, and specifically, the damaging effects of lightning.

After the storm, several business owners made a smart move: they installed lightning
rods. In case you're not familiar with them, lightning rods are metal strips or rods,
usually made of copper, used to protect buildings or structures from a violent
lightning strike. The lightning rod is connected by a cable to the earth below, where
it can channel the charge to a safe place. These rods are placed atop roofs to attract
lightning and protect buildings from lightning strikes. In fact, they are needed most
on structures that are tall or isolated. You see, lightning has a tendency to strike
whatever is nearest or at the highest elevation.

This thing called a lightning rod was invented by none other than Benjamin
Franklin. In fact, he experimented with these rods or "attractors" long before his
famous experiment with the key and the kite. Franklin knew the metal in those rods
would attract the lightning if they were up high enough, and they could spare the
building any damage. He got them working during his lifetime and by the 19th
century, lightning rods were popular and ornate, a symbol of American ingenuity.

Lightning rods are a picture of another leadership principle. Leaders operate like
lightning rods. They naturally attract light and heat from others. They are most
likely to be criticized when things go wrong, blamed if things don't get fixed, and
honored if things go well. When a storm hits, they take the light and heat for the
team. Both the perks and the price of leadership is recognition. People look to you.
The downside of this is criticism. People vent their anger on leaders. If you're

leading others, you'll be criticized and attacked. Just be ready. President Harry Truman said, "If you can't stand the heat, stay out of the kitchen." The key is to ground the heat in a positive way.

I don't know of any leader who did this better than President Abraham Lincoln. It's likely that no president in American history received such criticism and dishonor, sometimes from those who worked closest to him. Lincoln received much grief and bitterness from War Secretary Stanton. Once, a clerk asked President Lincoln what he thought of Stanton. Lincoln said he felt he was a good leader, straightforward, and almost always right. The clerk looked at him and said, "Mr. President, do you know that Mr. Stanton thinks you are an ape and criticizes you as a fool every chance he gets? How could you say such a thing?" President Lincoln just smiled at the clerk and replied, "You didn't ask me what Stanton thought of me. You asked what I thought of Mr. Stanton."[1]

Lincoln kept a level head and didn't strike back. He took the heat for his team several times when Southerners lashed out at his cabinet. During the Civil War, Lincoln once encouraged a general to attack, but the general feared losing his reputation if the battle didn't go well. Lincoln then did the unthinkable. He wrote the general and said, "I want you to go on the offense. If the battle goes well, you can take all the credit for victory. If it doesn't go well, I will take the blame completely."[2]

Lincoln also found a way to build lightning rods in his own leadership, places where he could vent and not damage team members. When angry with someone, Lincoln would occasionally write a hot letter to them. Then, he would set it aside until he cooled down. Inevitably, he would never send it. He had a drawer of angry letters he never sent.[3]

DEALING WITH CRITICISM

Here are some suggestions on handling criticism and becoming a good lightning rod:

A. UNDERSTAND THE DIFFERENCE BETWEEN CONSTRUCTIVE AND DESTRUCTIVE CRITICISM.

(Do they want to help you or hurt you? Can you see that anything good can come from it?)

B. RECOGNIZE THAT PEOPLE ACT OUT WHAT THEY ARE EXPERIENCING INSIDE. IT MAY NOT BE ABOUT YOU.

(Hurting people naturally hurt people. Intimidated people intimidate. What's inside comes out.)

C. REMEMBER THAT GOOD PEOPLE GET CRITICIZED.

(Some of the finest leaders in history were attacked. You're in good company.)

D. Don't just see the critic, see the crowd.

(Don't let minority rule. Are others feeling the same way as the critic or is the critic isolated?)

E. Eat the fish and spit out the bones.

(Digest the criticism and act on anything that's accurate. Improve what you can. Discard the rest.)

F. Wait for time to prove them wrong.

(Lincoln's "Gettysburg Address" was considered shameful and poorly written at the time.)

G. Act, don't react. Don't get defensive.

(Don't let their emotion dictate yours. Thank them for their opinions. Take the high road.)

H. Seek wise counsel from others.

(Consult with other leaders to see what kernels of truth might be in the criticism.)

I. Concentrate on your mission; change your mistakes.

(Many leaders get so frazzled when criticized that they do the opposite.)

One last insight: When a storm occurs and lightning does strike in your organization, fires of conflict can begin burning. Remember, you and every team member carry two buckets with you: a bucket of water and a bucket of gasoline. You can either throw gasoline on the fire and make it worse with a negative attitude, or you can throw water on it and put the fire out.

Some years ago, I watched a documentary on television that was an unforgettable illustration of this. Michael Weisser and Larry Trapp lived in the same town outside of Lincoln, Nebraska in the early 1990s. Michael noticed there were many people of other ethnicities moving into town who weren't getting connected to the local network. So he began to create welcome baskets for them. He knew they were feeling like outsiders, since most of the locals were not African American, Asian, or Hispanic.

Larry Trapp was the Grand Dragon of the local Ku Klux Klan. He stood for everything opposed to what Michael Weisser was doing. He was anonymously calling those people who were new in town and demanding that they leave town, or there would be hell to pay. He would threaten their lives if they didn't move out. When Larry Trapp heard what Michael Weisser was doing with the welcome baskets, he decided to call him… and threaten his life.

Michael returned home one night to hear this threat on his telephone answering machine. Hmmm. Do you know how he responded? Instead of fueling the conflict, he never even called the police. He decided every telephone call deserved a call back. So, he did some homework on who might have made such a call (it didn't take him long to figure it out; Larry Trapp had a reputation in town). Michael called Larry back. This is what he said: "Larry, it's Michael Weisser. I got your phone call." Then, without making any mention of the threat, he went on. "I wanted you to know that I did some homework on you and heard that you were a diabetic. And, I heard that you were confined to a wheelchair. (Both of these statements were true.) I just got to thinking that maybe someone like you could use the help of someone like me. You see, I have a big van, and I would be glad to drive over, pick you up, and run some errands for you if you ever need that. What do you say?"

Larry Trapp was stunned. He was quiet for a few moments. Then, he mustered the words, "No thank you... but, thank you for the offer. I have never been offered anything like that before." As fate would have it, the next day, Larry called Michael back and took him up on his offer. These two men began spending time together over the next several weeks. These two became friends, which led to Larry Trapp's resignation from the Klan and his public denouncement of all he had done with them. Larry Trapp ended up moving in with Michael, where he stayed until he eventually died from his diabetic complications. But it wasn't until that town had been transformed by one leader who acted instead of reacting. Michael Weisser was a lightning rod. He took the heat and grounded it.

REFLECT AND RESPOND

Lightning rods and leaders have something in common—they take the heat in the midst of storms. Leaders are honored when things go right, but they also are blamed when things go wrong. The key for a leader to positively handle criticism is to become a good lightning rod, to learn how to channel the impact to a safe place.

1. President Lincoln is a positive example of a leader who knew how to take the heat for his team. What can we learn from him? How did he act like a lightning rod? How did he vent his anger and not damage his team members?

_____

_____

_____

_____

2. Do you agree with the suggestion that people act out what they are experiencing inside? Have you ever experienced the truth of the phrase, "hurting people naturally hurt people?" If so, describe how you handled it.

_____

_____

_____

_____

_____

3. In the analogy that each of us chooses to carry one of two kinds of buckets, which kind of bucket do you carry? Are you more likely to throw gasoline on the fire by a bad attitude? Or react in anger? Or do you typically carry a bucket of water to help put out the fire?

_____

_____

_____

_____

Self-Assessment

Evaluate yourself on this issue of anger and acting as a lightning rod for others:

	Yes	No
1. Do I get defensive and retaliate when criticized?	___	___
2. Does my anger cause me to seek revenge?	___	___
3. Does flattery or criticism affect me too much?	___	___
4. Is it hard for me to see or welcome kernels of truth in criticism?	___	___
5. Can I remain objective and poised when attacked?	___	___
6. Do I channel my emotions toward a solution?	___	___
7. Can I take the heat for my team and not complain?	___	___
8. Do I have a place to vent my own anger as a leader?	___	___

(Healthy leaders can say "no" to the first four and "yes" to the last four. How did you do?)

EXERCISE

This week, be on the lookout for criticism and heat from others. (I know that sounds crazy—but watch for it.) Then, look for ways you can take the heat for the team. Identify ways you can resolve the conflict and bring peace and cooperation to the team again. Get creative.

Next, find people who can be accountability partners for you on this issue. Gather one or two people that you can "vent" with, and share your hurts and even anger in a healthy way. Be sure they are not people who might be negatively affected by your anger because they serve on your team. Find times to meet with them and ground your anger so you can lead in a positive way.

The Poet's Gift

POETS ARE STUDENTS OF THEIR CULTURE AND GRAB THE HEARTS OF READERS BY EXPRESSING IDEAS IN RELEVANT AND CREATIVE WAYS. LIKEWISE, LEADERS INTERPRET THE LANDSCAPE BEFORE THEY COMMUNICATE. THEY INTERPRET BEFORE THEY INFORM; THEY READ BEFORE THEY LEAD. THIS MAKES FOR RELEVANT COMMUNICATION.

I distinctly remember reading poetry in my freshman literature class in college. In fact, I remember reading poetry from my high school and middle school years, too. William Shakespeare, Robert Frost, Edgar Allen Poe, and so many others have been indelibly etched in my mind. The other day, a friend asked me a question which took me back to those days in college, and I remembered one of my favorite poems. Without a second thought, I cited "The Road Less Traveled" perfectly, word for word. It scared me.

Why was I able to remember that poem? Let's reflect for a moment. Can you remember your favorite poem or song lyrics from high school or some other critical period in your life? Why is it that years later the poem still stands out in your mind? Author Lystra Richardson suggests that one reason is because some aspect of that poem resonated with you at an emotional level. I agree. The word "poetry" comes from a Greek term. It describes a written art form in which language is used for its aesthetic qualities in addition to its semantic content. The use of features like rhythm, rhyme, and meter elicit emotion and make it memorable.

Poetry as an art form pre-dates literacy. In other words, people were citing poetry before they could read it. Poetry was employed as a means of recording oral history, storytelling, genealogy, and law. Poetry speaks to our heart and it is said in a memorable way.

Leaders, like poets, are required to rise above the fray of the everyday to inspire and encourage the human heart. In a very real sense, leaders are poets. They communicate vision in a memorable way and folks remember it when they're done. The word "poet" is taken from a root word meaning "I create." Poets don't create something out of nothing, however. It's quite the opposite. Poets read and interpret the culture around them, and then they put words to what they see. This is what effective leaders do as well. They are listeners, and they are wordsmiths. After President Gerald Ford finished his term in office, he was asked what he would do differently if he could do it all over again. He replied, "I would go back to school and learn to communicate better."

Probably the most famous speech of the 20th century was made by a black pastor from Atlanta, Georgia. His name was Dr. Martin Luther King, Jr. We remember the speech as "I Have a Dream." As I travel worldwide, I've found that more people know that speech than any other. Think for a moment what made that speech so effective. Let me suggest a few items:

1. He repeated the phrase "I have a dream" several times to drive his point home.

2. He was inclusive, taking his audience all over the U.S. with his words.

3. He used familiar metaphors to describe what he meant.

4. He was relevant, since he spoke from society's needs and concerns.

5. He identified with them, speaking of marching and going to prison together.

6. He gave the people a point for their heads and a picture for their hearts.

That speech is memorable because King utilized these tools as he spoke. What you may not know is that Dr. King took a hand-written manuscript up to the podium that day that was scheduled to last 11 minutes. When he finished it, however, he intuitively knew his audience had not caught the big idea; they didn't get the "a-ha." So he began to speak from the overflow of his years of learning, using the phrase "I have a dream." He went a total of 17 minutes. When he sat down, he did so only after reading the faces of the people and realizing he had gotten the job done. He was a poet that day. He read the culture, he read the faces of his audience, then he led effectively.

LEARNING FROM POETS

Leaders can learn much from great poets. Ultimately, they add value by interpreting their world, summarizing an idea, and using a "hook" to share it in a memorable fashion. Hooks enable people to grab ideas. (Dr. King's "hook" was his repeated phrase "I Have a Dream.") Poet-leaders utilize simplicity, accuracy, imagery, and relevance. They simplify because they want to impact people, not impress them. Poet-leaders search for the right word and use an economy with words. They don't give in to the need to "tell all." They exercise restraint. Accuracy is about selecting the precise word rather than adding all the words that could possibly be used. Poets and leaders search for the uncommon word that conjures up both logic and emotion. Imagery makes abstract ideas concrete. Using images, analogies, or pictures helps the listener grab the idea. (It's what we try to do with these *Habitudes*!)

Finally, relevance is about observing before communicating. Think about a college quarterback who calls for an option play. As he stands at the line ready to take the snap, he is reading several factors to know what to do next. He reads the defense, the clock, the field position, the talent he has around him, and the yards his team needs for a first down. Then, taking the snap, he uses one of three options: he can throw the ball downfield, he can lateral the ball to a halfback, or he can keep it and run. What he does is all determined by reading the situation before he acts. This enables him to lead in a relevant manner.

In one sense, Prime Minister Winston Churchill was a poet as he led England during World War II. He read the situation, then used five ingredients when he spoke during that dark period of Britain's history. We can summarize Churchill's secrets of effective communication with these five tools:[1]

1. STRONG BEGINNING

He didn't waste time with small talk. He plunged right into his message with a provocative story, quote, statement, or fact. He engaged the audience immediately with a relevant thought.

2. ONE THEME

He didn't try to share too many points, just one. He had one central vision or message he wished to convey in each talk. Less is more was his mindset. Often you could boil it down to one phrase.

3. SIMPLE LANGUAGE

He didn't try to impress anyone with big words. He spoke the everyday language of conversations. He didn't care about his image. He didn't care about impressing folks. He spoke for impact.

4. PICTURES

He created colorful images in people's minds. He was an artist with word pictures, stories, and metaphors. These illustrated his point and made it memorable. They were his "hooks."

5. EMOTIONAL ENDING

He concluded by engaging their emotions, not just their minds. He would give them a call to action. He elicited powerful hunger by grabbing their hearts with a personal plea to engage in his vision.

Reflect and Respond

There's no doubt about it: leaders should learn how to communicate from good poets. Poets touch the hearts of their readers in creative and relevant ways. Leaders must learn to read their followers before they can effectively lead.

1. Describe the qualities that good leaders and poets share. What do we learn about relevant communication from poets?

_____

_____

_____

_____

_____

2. Dr. Martin Luther King, Jr. became famous for his "I Have a Dream" speech. What were some of the factors that made his speech so effective and memorable?

_____

_____

_____

_____

_____

3. Poet-leaders utilize four essentials in their communication: simplicity, accuracy, imagery and relevance. Explain what you learned about these four elements as they relate to being a poet-leader.

_____

_____

_____

_____

4. What's the most important goal a leader can have when he or she speaks to the team?

_____

_____

_____

_____

5. How do you stay relevant when you speak to your team?

_____

_____

_____

_____

_____

SELF-ASSESSMENT

Take a minute to evaluate your own communication. Are you a poet for others?

1. I read people and situations, then speak in a relevant way.

< POOR 1 2 3 4 5 6 7 8 9 10 EXCELLENT >

2. I am skilled at putting memorable words to ideas.

< POOR 1 2 3 4 5 6 7 8 9 10 EXCELLENT >

3. I inspire others to act through the words I speak.

< POOR 1 2 3 4 5 6 7 8 9 10 EXCELLENT >

4. I am a student of the culture around me and speak to its needs.

< POOR 1 2 3 4 5 6 7 8 9 10 EXCELLENT >

EXERCISE

Examine the needs around you that are relevant to your team or organization. Choose one of those needs and reflect on the real issue at hand. Listen to others around you and size up what they are saying about the need. Then, take some time and identify what could be done to solve the problem. When you've formed an idea, put it into memorable words. Next, create a talk that casts vision for what could be done. Follow the five tools that Winston Churchill used: strong beginning, one theme, simple language, pictures, and emotional ending. What single thought do you want to leave with your team? When it's appropriate, share this little talk with your team or organization. Evaluate how they respond to you as a "poet."

[End Notes]

IMAGE ONE: HOSTS AND GUESTS

[1] Jones, JoAnn C., "A Most Important Question," *Guideposts*, July 1996, 8.

IMAGE TWO: THE INDIAN TALKING STICK

[1] Robert S. McNamara with Brian VanDeMark, *In Retrospect: The Tragedy and Lessons of Vietnam* (New York: Vintage, 1996).

IMAGE THREE: CHESS AND CHECKERS

[1] Marcus Buckingham, *The One Thing You Need to Know...About Great Managing, Great Leading, and Sustained Individual Success* (New York, NY: Free Press, 2005), 81-125.

[2] Captain D. Michael Abrashoff, *It's Your Ship.* (New York, NY: Warner Books, 2002), 48-49.

IMAGE FOUR: THE CALCUTTA PARADOX

[1] Renzo Allegri, *Mother Theresa: The Early Years*, August 1996, <http://www.ewtn.com/library/ISSUES/EARLYYR.HTM>

[2] Jim Collins, *Good to Great*, (New York, NY: HarperCollins, 2001), 27-30, 33-35.

IMAGE SIX: HOT AIR BALLOONS

[1] Tom Rath and Donald O. Clifton, Ph.D., *How Full is Your Bucket? Positive Strategies for Work and Life* (New York, NY: Gallup Press, 2004), 17-24.

[2] ibid, 39.

[3] ibid, 25.

[4] Abrashoff, *It's Your Ship*, 144.

[5] Thomas Peters and Nancy Austin, *A Passion for Excellence* (New York, NY: Warner Books, 1985), 297.

IMAGE SEVEN: THE VELVET COVERED BRICK

1 Chip Bell and Bilijack Bell, *Magnetic Service: Secrets of Creating Passionately Devoted Customers* (San Francisco, CA: Berrett-Koehler Publishers, 2003).

2 Lubell, Sam. "No Pink Slip. You're Just Dot-Gone." *New York Times* 150, no. 51696 (03/18/2001): 2.

3 Doris Kearns Goodwin, "The Master of the Game," *Time*, July 2005, vol. 166.

IMAGE EIGHT: POCKET CHANGE

1 Oren Harari and Lynn Brewer, "If Colin Powell had Commanded Enron: the Hidden Foundation of Leadership," *Business Strategy Review*, Summer 2004, vol. 15, 40.

2 Rick Reilly, *A Paragon Rising Above the Madness*, March 14, 2000, <http://sportsillustrated.cnn.com/inside_game/magazine/life_of_reilly/news/2000/03/14/life_of_reilly/>

IMAGE TEN: THE GARDENER'S JOB

1 Eliza G.C. Collins and Patricia Scott, "Everyone Who Makes it has a Mentor," *Harvard Business Review*, July/August 1978.

IMAGE ELEVEN: TIGHTROPE WALKER

1 William Beausay II, *The Leadership Genius of Jesus: Ancient Wisdom for Modern Business* (Nashville, TN: Thomas Nelson, 1997), 116-117.

2 *Declining Levels of Employee Trust are a Major Threat to Corporate Competitiveness*, Watson Wyatt Study Finds, July 25 2002. <http://www.watsonwyatt.com/news/press.asp?ID=10221>

3 James Garlow, *The 21 Irrefutable Laws of Leadership Tested by Time* (Nashville, TN: Thomas Nelson, 2002), 16-20.

IMAGE TWELVE: LIGHTNING RODS

1 Goodwin, "The Master of the Game."

2 ibid.

3 ibid.

IMAGE THIRTEEN: THE POET'S GIFT

1 James C. Humes, *The Sir Winston Method: The Five Secrets of Speaking the Language of Leadership* (New York, NY: William Morrow and Company, 1991).

Acknowledgements

A great team worked together on this book. My thanks goes to Dave Mierau, who spearheaded a team of researchers including Drew Flamm and Tabitha Dixon. I also am grateful to Anne Alexander for proofing the manuscript, and to Brad Scholle for overseeing the logistics of the book. Finally, thanks to the Growing Leaders team who incarnates the principles in this book. I love you guys.

Tim Elmore